WITHDRAWN
NDSU

Independence My Way

Independence My Way

Kaizer D. Matanzima

FAA

Published by the Foreign Affairs Association, 936 Pretorius Street, Pretoria.

ISBN   0 908397 05 4

Copyright © 1976 by Foreign Affairs Association

All rights reserved by the publishers. No portion of this book may be reproduced in any way without written permission from the publisher except by a reviewer, who may quote brief passages in connection with a review.

Printed by Colorpress (Pty) Ltd.

CONTENTS

The Goat's Skin Days	1
The Case for Independence	19
My Uphill Battle for Political Rights	39
Emergence of Two Parties	57
Blazing a Trail for Black Recognition	72
Terrorism, Communism and other Issues	87
My land and its People	107
My Great Love — Education	126
Quotes by Paramount Chief Matanzima	137

LIST OF PHOTOGRAPHS

Coastal Landscape	5
Rural Scene	9
Port St Johns	15
Men with their traditional long-stemmed pipes	25
Pondos gather to drink beer	33
The Bunga in Umtata	41
Ex-President J J Fouché delivering the opening address to the Legislative Assembly in 1971	47
Umtata's new skyline	61
The Town Hall with the Government Building in the background	67
Magwa Waterfall	77
Xhosa woman with traditional long-stemmed pipe	83
Chief Minister K D Matanzima	89
Traditional beadwork	111
Tea plantation, Transkei	115
Forestry was started in 1904	119
Hillmond textile factory	123
Jongilizwe School for Sons of Chiefs at Tsolo	131

1

the goat's skin days

I was born on June 15, 1915 at Qamata in the St Marks district. My parents named me Kaizer Daliwonga Matanzima.

Why *Kaizer?* To understand how I was given my first name, you have to remember that it was at the time of the First World War. My parents, simple people from the deeply carved valleys of my birthplace, far away from the holocaust in Europe, were not unaware of the world leaders striding the world scene in those momentous times. So I was duly christened Kaizer after the Emperor of Germany. For his part my younger brother, George, the present Minister of Justice, was named after King George V of Great Britain.

In spite of the illustrious names given to my brother and myself, my life in those early days was merely that of a herdboy, although my father, Chief Mhlobo Mvuzo Matanzima Mtirara, was the Chief of Emigrant Tembuland. There were hardly any schools in the vicinity of Qamata at the time. Members of the community were all illiterate. Only my father had been to an educational institution—and he only went up to Standard Four. My mother, Mogedi, had received no education whatsoever.

My parents had great ideals for me—and later for my younger brother, George. They must have looked at their two sons, clad in sheepskin called "goat's vel", and decided: "These two will have to learn, learn, learn ..." The first step, therefore, was to send me to school. My father, especially, insisted upon this. I think it must have been a great day for him when I was enrolled at the local school. I attach great sentimental value to this event, because it was my father's school. Yes, my father ran a school where he paid the teachers himself. Their pay was taken from his own remuneration as Chief. The female teacher in that school, I remember, was Nomeytshi. This school is today called the Mhlobo School—named after my father.

In 1922 I was sent to a neighbouring location where I attended classes at the Ntlonze Primary School up to Standard Three. My father then sent me to a respectable Chief in the district under his jurisdiction, Chief Falo Mgudlwa, where I passed Standard Four in the Qumanco Higher Primary School. In those days I was usually accompanied by an old man called Willie Moni (Umzokola). Many week-ends we rode to and from Qumanco on horseback.

My intense love for my country springs from those "goat's vel" days in the rolling hills of places like Qumanco and Qamata. Forests, trees and rippling water over stones and sand became part of my young soul. The seeds for the other great love in my life—education—were probably also sown subconsciously in those carefree days of my youth. Even now I often reflect with quiet gratitude—and modest pride—on the fact that I was instrumental in the establishment in 1950 of the first Secondary School for my tribe, namely the Matanzima Secondary School at Cala in the Xalanga district. I was also instrumental in launching additional classes for another tribal school which is known as Rhoda Secondary School at Wodehouse Forest in the St Marks district.

It was a humble beginning, but sometimes greatness is built upon just such beginnings ...

But, to return to those days which now seem to belong to the long distant past. I was at Qumanco for one year only. The year 1930 dawned. I was now nearly 15 years old, and my father had more ambitious dreams for my future. He set hig sights on Lovedale, the great Missionary Institution for Blacks at Alice in the Eastern Cape, which is named after Dr John Love, at the time Secretary of the Glasgow Missionary Society. My father applied for my admission to

Lovedale. It was accepted and I passed Standards Five and Six under Mr Wesley Caley, Principal of the Lovedale School.

Whilst at Lovedale, tragedy struck our family. My father, the man who did everything in his power to place my feet on the first rungs of the ladder to the top, passed away in 1932. For me it was a heavy blow, but I was inspired by his memory to try and reach the ideals he awakened in me from my earliest youth. According to our tribal system, I, as the hereditary Chief of Emigrant Tembuland, was placed under the guardianship of my uncle, Mr Dalubuhle Matanzima, who was appointed as Regent. I was under the guardianship of my uncle for eight years.

In 1933 I was awarded the Andrew Smith bursary for three years' further study. After attaining my Junior Certificate in 1934 at Lovedale, my tribesmen, on the recommendation of Mr McLoughlin, at the time Native Commissioner for St Marks district, decided that I should further my studies at Fort Hare (then called The College) at their expense. In 1936 I passed the Matriculation Examination and in 1939 I obtained a B.A. degree from the University of South Africa, majoring in Roman Law and Political Science.

Something about the spirit of those days—my tender youth and the later period at Loveday and Fort Hare—was recalled at my 60th birthday party at my home at Qamata on June 22, 1975. In the presence of many guests, amongst them many of my old school friends, my brother George, the present Minister of Justice, said inter alia:

> *It's a great pleasure to narrate his life history. Although I am younger than my brother, I am the only one who can describe it. I doubt if those who lived in these areas in 1915 were aware then that it was the first chapter in an historical book that would one day be read in the Transkei, South Africa and the rest of the world. That's exactly what has happened. These contemporaries, I believe, saw me daily walking and playing with this young boy who always wore a sheepskin, like myself. The skins, incidentally, gave much warmth to the wearer.*

> *In 1933 K D obtained the covetous Andrew Smith bursary. This bursary had a very high status and was obtained only by the best selectees in the Cape. Among his contemporaries at Lovedale were Nese Tsotsi and myself. In those days, I'm afraid, our English was still on the rusty side. I now know that my elder brother was not so very good in English. He knew more arithmetic than the rest. I am told that one morning he was sent to borrow a shoe-brush from a senior and was obliged to speak English.*
>
> *He said: 'You have a brush for red shoes?' (Meaning: have you a red shoe-brush?)*
>
> *The answer was naturally 'Yes, we have.' And Mr Kobus, you see over there, in sympathy said, 'Yes you may have mine, sonny', with a suppressed laughter.*

In my speech that day I also referred to our Fort Hare days: "We were all rather known for seriousness about education. A favourite pastime was to speak elaborate English. We were expected to speak English throughout the week in those days (King's English). But there was also inevitable howling. A certain Mr Ngamlana—now a Headman down our way—was forced one day to tell us how he was punished by Major Geddes for saying when reporting a thrashing event as *That boy, Sir, was throwing me by stones; I now come to report him to the big master.*"

I also reminisced about the earlier days: "Honourable Ministers, Chiefs, friends from various places—Umtata, Qumbu, Engcobo, Kentani, Butterworth, Ladysmith, King William's Town, East London—I'm rather sad to observe that my ancestral Chiefs never reached the age of 60, even father Mhlontlo! Of them all, only my grandfather lived to that age. Yes, Matanzima did, Mtirara's son. I had invited my equals only to this party, but now it seems that people from all walks of life have come. We were just going to have a chat. This also proves that the people love me; they were all the more determined to come even if uninvited. My contemporaries are here.

"Rev Bolani used to narrate how we as boys would sit and chat; later we would say to the younger boys: *'Go home, your*

Coastal landscape

money is finished now. Your fun money is finished—only big boys should remain.' That was our excuse for starting a fight. This I'm reminded of by this day.

"I met Mr R Peteni, who proposed the toast to me, outside here and I said to him that this is not the day for small boys —I was referring to his younger brother who was with him and is today a medical doctor himself. I do not know whether the doctor liked that remark!

"On this day I remember some of the people I used to play with as youngsters at Lovedale: Rev de Wall Mahlasela is one; Mr Peteni is here, my equal; here I see Gladstone Msuthu (Std 5 colleague)—our common trainer being Mr Moahloli who would say to us *'Touch your toes'*. Another popular girl of the time was Norma—where is she? She was very young then but she eventually yielded and agreed to marry me.

"I was at school with these people. There were also those who were seniors to me: Mr Makhohliso, Lujabe (not this small boy here). The chaps were always well-dressed: fish-tails, Oxford bags (the present bell-bottoms), three buttons, etc. These were the fashions of the day. Lovedale taught us how to appear smart. You could not be allowed to go to the dining hall without a tie (I hope the boarding master of Rhoda is listening). No tie, no food! But there were days we were allowed to share the dining rooms with the ladies.

"At Fort Hare I also met Geoffrey Kakana, the pianist and composer and student. He composed a song we have not forgotten even today: lampooning a number of people at Fort Hare: the lazy, the bright, the frail and the morally weak. The song was composed on Kakana's having passed his Matriculation (a feat in those days). He used to play the piano every day, much to the pleasure of our dancing feet. Sam Bikitsha used to bully me into making tea for him. I, in turn, cheated Siwisa, or Columbus Funani. Sam wanted me to be on call at times to make his tea, to talk to him or run errands for him to Miss Francis Mvambo. We were happy, and besides we were learning. There were hardly any strikes. We were concerned solely with our learning."

On that happy occasion I also referred to my mother: "My mother did not know or guess when she bore me that a Transkei leader was being born. She did not know anything about education. She came here red-blanketed. I say red because in those days there were no other blankets but red ones in these parts. The blankets were dyed red with red-ochre, and all women wore red blankets. That's how they were trained—a red blanket and the taste of the sjambok every day! Hence my mother knew how to rear us in the atmosphere of the hard way of life. I'm proud of it— she saw to it that we did not become 'softies'. It was my brother George, my sister, now Mrs Somdyala, and myself."

And my wife: "I wish to introduce my wife—the one that brought an assegai and stuck it into the ground; the national mother of all. I hunted all over for a suitable wife after I left school. All the girls in this area were red-blanketed. I could not see my way clear to marrying in these areas. So I asked Nelson Mandela to find me a wife. The girl I eventually married came from the Santoni's in Qokolweni, on the side of the river where there was no witchcraft. And indeed she was a sparkling beauty. I am also grateful to her for having good helpers, my other wives."

Mr R Peteni, the toastmaster, had this to say:

I am really pleased to have this privilege of speaking on this occasion. I feel small and humble to address such a noble gathering: my elders, equals and superiors. We used to play with some of them as children: balloon-ball, grappling with one another, chasing around, etc. With Chief K D we used to play ball. At times there were fights, but we always remained friends; we would still go to the girls' hostel together! Chief K D and I used to call each other 'swaer' (brother-in-law) for no special reason. This continues even today. I once met him at Johannesburg's Park Station and when he saw me he shouted 'Sibali!' I did not know what to say. How can I shout 'Sibali' to a Chief Minister? I mumbled a few words, but I could not say 'Hello Chief Minister', nor 'Sibali'. No matter where you

> meet him—here, or abroad, he remains the same man. I'm sure he would have done that even when he left the rostrum of the UNO (he attended the meeting of the world body as an observer with the South African delegation in 1974)—if he saw me he still would say 'Sibali'.

In a more serious vein Mr Peteni continued:

> Now to come to another point: it is providence that at this time and place he is called upon to lead the Transkei and be its chosen leader. He leads the Transkei and his leadership is evident everywhere as you travel through this land. As we stand up to toast his life, we simultaneously propose a toast to the Transkei and each person in the Transkei—you and you and you. Every Black person shines in the glory and success of the Transkei as well as those in the Republic. If the Transkei fails, everybody will have failed; what hurts the Transkei, hurts everybody, every Black man ...

So the memory of our youth lives on in the hearts of my contemporaries and myself. But, to return to my career.

In 1940, after obtaining the B.A. degree, I returned home. If I am not mistaken, I was the first Chief in the country to obtain a degree. In June of that year I was appointed Chief of the Ama-Hala clan of the Tembu's in the St Marks district. In passing, I may mention that the rulers at the time did not attach great importance to a degree. And the best way to control a chief who thought he was educated was to starve him—give him a starving wage! I earned £8 per month at the time, and later on my brother George, with his B.Sc. degree, received the princely sum of £11 per month.

The desire, however, burned in me to serve my people, the Tembu people. I wanted to serve the nation. I continued making representations to the South African Government for recognition as Regional Chief of Emigrant Tembuland. (This was finally granted in 1958). In 1942 I was nominated by the Government and became a member of the United Transkeian Territories General Council (UTTGC), that is the old Bunga.

I noticed that seating arrangements in the Bunga were

Rural scene

such that the magistrates sat around in a horse-shoe and the Chiefs were seated in such a way as to be under the scrutiny of the respective magistrates—and one dares not deviate from the beaten track! A swinging action of the seat of a magistrate was enough to discipline or control any recalcitrant Chief at the back. I soon became convinced that this status of a leader, that is being a stooge to a magistrate, means little to the leadership of a Chief. My entire nature revolted against such leadership. In actual fact the magistrate was the real Chief; the Black Chief was merely a dummy. If a Chief failed to attend any quarterly meeting, his pay was immediately suspended until he explained his absence satisfactorily. That is why I was determined to dissolve the Bunga; from the outset I regarded it as an obsolete thing. So I resigned from the Bunga in 1944 and decided to take study leave in order to study law.

I assumed duty as an articled clerk to a firm of attorneys, Hemming & Hemming, in Umtata, subsequently known as Hemming and Hughes, in order to prepare for the attorney's admission examination. (The latter refers to Mr Gray Hughes, who represented the Natives of the Transkei in terms of the 1939 legislation.) I passed the entrance examination of the Cape of Good Hope Law Society with honours in 1948. I attained the highest marks in the Cape and won the Cape Law Society's prize of law books worth £10. After passing my attorney's admission examination, I did not practise as a lawyer.

I think it is true to say that I took up law to gain more knowledge for my calling—that of Chief of my people and leader of my people. I was granted jurisdiction to try civil claims arising between members of my tribe at the Great Place at Qamata. I started building court houses and occupied myself with court work. It was one of the first innovations amongst the Chiefs to built court houses in order to try cases according to modern methods. And fortunately with my law certificate it was not difficult to deal with these cases according to tribal customs.

In 1955 I again became a member of the General Council

of the United Transkei Areas, not with the aim of co-operating with it but with the object of killing it. Let me explain.

The National Party came into power in 1948, which was a controversial year for South Africa. In 1951 the Bantu Authorities Act was promulgated, and I realised that this legislation laid the foundation for the eventual independence of the African people. So when I became a member of the UTTGC in 1955 I sought my opportunity to lobby in the House and to make friends among the members. This council and its 26 district councils was subsequently dissolved in 1956 and was replaced by the Transkeian Territorial Authority under the Bantu Authorities System. This made provision for the introduction of a Territorial Authority plus Regional, District and Tribal or Community authorities.

I served on the committee drafting the Transkeian Territorial Bantu Authorities Proclamation, which later became law. By virtue of this Proclamation, I automatically became the permanent Regional Chief of the Emigrant Tembu districts of St Marks and Xalanga and therewith a member of the TTA and its Executive Committee. I regard the proclamation of the Bantu Self-Government Act in 1959 as a milestone because it was a further step in the direction of nation-building and independence.

In 1961 I was elected to succeed Paramount Chief Botha Sigcau, the first Chairman of the Bantu Authorities in the Transkei, as Chairman of the TTA—by implication the leader of my people. In this capacity I attended the inauguration of Advocate C R Swart as the first State President of the Republic of South Africa on May 31, 1961. I was, therefore, the last Chairman of the now defunct TTA. In this capacity I also played a major role in the compilation of the draft constitution which culminated in the Transkei Constitution of 1963, and thus the development of the Homeland as a self-governing territory.

And now, after almost 12 years of self-government and on the eve of independence, I have the utmost confidence in the future of my country. I am looking forward to the exciting task of leading my people to full independence. But on this road to independence, I had to overcome many serious obstacles, even to the extent of threats on my life. My brother George touched on some of these on the occasion of my 60th birthday. In referring to my role in those sometimes anxious times, he referred to Whites with Communistic leanings who used to fan artificial fires, and to angry Blacks who were yelling for my blood. Continuing, George said:

> *Who can risk his life so many times and still be called a stooge? And the loudest of the dissident people are those who are idle, low-geared and who have contributed nothing for any cause or nation! All they know is to crawl like snakes and howl like dogs.*
>
> *After the Promotion of Self-Government Act of 1959, a further milestone on the road to independence, all kinds of pet names were given to this move: an attempt to create Bantustans or Homelands (whatever kind of land that is). But the name given, is beside the point. What really matters is what one hopes to achieve. Since the Bantu Authorities Proclamation of 1956 I was, and still am, very close to Paramount Chief K D and his philosophy. I realised that this would be better than the Bunga, which degenerated into Bungu (the rot). My brother K D does not normally cry: 'I'll do so and so, and so and so.' He knows exactly what his next move will be. You will note that when he contemplates his next major step, he becomes pensive. The next thing you see is a big step forward, undertaken in his usual fearless manner.*
>
> *That is the way K D acts. He is like a traditional stick-fighter who defends himself and at the appropriate moment stands on one leg, collects himself and fells the enemy with one single blow. At one time, I remember, K D was away in Cape Town. In his absence, plots of sabotage against him were brewing. Many Whites with leftist leanings were antagonistic towards him. I am not sure what happened—all of a sudden many of these White civil servants resigned their jobs one by one. I could not contain myself any longer so I took*

my car and drove to meet K D halfway to tell him the news that his enemies had suddenly resigned and were leaving the Transkei!

You all realise that there is no nation on earth which does not crave independence. At the same time, there is also no human being who does not want his freedom. The only possible difference is the method of achieving independence. Arrive at your destination first and then, and only then, can you say: 'This is the way it is done.' Your invitation should be: Come let us enjoy the fruits of freedom, the fruits of independence. You cannot criticise anyone until you are in a position to prove some success of achievement attained on your own part.

In order to see the abovementioned in its proper perspective, I have to turn back the clock even further. I saw South Africa grow. The year of Union, 1910, is not such a long time before the year of my birth. When General Louis Botha was Prime Minister of the Union of South Africa, I was already a strapping youth. Then General J C Smuts took over. When General J B M Hertzog introduced the poll tax in 1924, I was already at school. In 1927 the Native Administration Act was passed. South Africa then belonged to the Whites only. Blacks were just like cattle on sale and the Black man's burden was to work for the Whites (as labourers).

In 1936, when the voting rights were taken away, I was at Fort Hare with others, intensely interested in what was happening. And when the late Professor Jabavu called for a National Convention at Bloemfontein, we were already active young men ready to face dusty roads and the hurly-burly ahead of us. Professor Jabavu that day delivered a marathon speech at Bloemfontein which inspired everybody. I left school at the end of 1939, three years after the withdrawal of the vote from Black persons. I am, therefore, fully acquainted with the constitutional development of the Republic of South Africa.

I left school convinced that I should have a part to play in the liberation of the Black in every field of life: equality in wages, in commerce, in fact everything. I was involved in the task of eliminating all discrimination in the Transkei. Salaries for medical doctors (Black and White) are equal today. We have since appointed our first young boys to train in the foreign service. Without advertising we were able to select all those graduates. They are to be trained as ambassadors and consuls. All this means that South Africa is changing, slowly changing, in an evolutionary manner.

The future is bright for the Transkei. All this has been accomplished in the face of opposition from people who have the temerity to call me a stooge of the South African Government! These are people who want to break down whatever has been built up by us at Umtata. We build, they destroy. In broader perspective I think it is true to say that we all seek peace and a solution to the international situation. But there is no peace; each nation wants to be better than the next—and there is no peace. I still want to boast that of all the nations in Africa, none will be better that the Transkei in polish and ambassadorial finish. Hence the very freedom we want must be civilised and polished.

But to return to the distant years of my youth. I was very fond of sport. Even today I like to attend rugby test matches, like the one I saw at the Free State Stadium in Bloemfontein between the Springboks and the All Blacks. My sporting activities included soccer, rugby, cricket and athletics (hurdles and the high jump). But my hobby, when I left school, was horse-riding. I didn't own a car at the time. I moved about among my subjects on horseback for eighteen years, so I managed to know them intimately, and they also knew me intimately. But now I travel by car and they don't see much of me.

In 1940 I got married and my first child, a son, was born. He was named Mthetwa, and he was heir to the Chieftainship. My son also graduated at Fort Hare and passed his law examination in 1968. The following year he was installed as Chief of the Nogayti region. He died in a car accident in 1972 when he was nearly 30. He was survived by his wife and a small son, who is now heir to the Chieftainship.

Port St Johns

I neither smoke nor drink, and I am a lay preacher in the Methodist Church. I am a religious man. I take the Republic of South Africa as my model. When the people approach me with the suggestion that we should have a casino, I invariably put the question: Why does the RSA not have a casino?

That then is a kaleidoscope of my life thus far. In the abovementioned I quoted quite extensively from what was said at Qamata during the commemoration of my 60th birthday. In all modesty, I am grateful for the kind words which were said about me on that occasion. In conclusion, I should like to say that in what I have achieved through my deeds to the benefit of the Transkei thus far, I was largely inspired by my intense love for my country and my people.

I hope that you will realise this when you read my speech when I introduced the Transkei Flag Bill. (This important milestone was reached when it was announced in Government Notice No 6 that the State President had assented to the Transkeian Flag Act, 1966. The Legislative Assembly of the Transkei approved the Act on May 5, 1966.) The Transkeian flag consists of three horizontal stripes of equal width. From the top down the stripes are ochre-red, white and green.

On that day I said that the flag was the symbol of the separate existence of the Xhosa-speaking people. I continued: "It was a symbol of our unity as a people and reflected our identity as a separate national group within the framework of South Africa. Through the grace of God we have become a nation with a home and a fatherland in the Transkei. We are now citizens of the Transkei and it is incumbent upon us to establish an outward visible symbol of our separate entity and of our own citizenship. A flag is a unifying factor, especially with us where we have various tribes. Without such a symbol of common citizenship to encourage us to reach for the heights and to inspire us to noble efforts, we cannot live, we cannot grow, we can never become a nation of any status.

Ochre-red

"The design of the flag was referred to a non-political committee. The committee had decided on the colours ochre-red, white and green. Ochre-red is without doubt the traditional colour of the Transkei. Im-bola, the general term for the various kinds of red clay or red ochre found in the Transkei, is still used by various tribes of the Transkei. There are two varieties of Imbola—the iCitywa and the uCumse. The iCitywa is used as a protection against the sun, as a cosmetic and for the decorating of homes and, lastly, as a protection against the bites of insects. The uCumse is used for colouring water apparel and to many Xhosa-speaking tribes it symbolises 'self'—thus once you apply it to your garment it (the ochre) joins, as it were, your 'personality'—it becomes 'you'.

"In this flag then the ochre-red is the traditional colour symbolising protection and self-realisation. Protection of all those rights a law-abiding citizen would justly expect the State to protect. That is protection against, as it were, the scorching rays of the sun by day and the biting cold by night; protection against hunger and thirst; protection of life and property and protection of all political and civil rights, whilst on the wings of the winds the further message of self-realisation will be carried through our fertile valleys and over our green undulating hills, a message which will reverberate for ever more: BE YOURSELF! Be proud to be yourself—a Xhosa-speaking people brought into existence by an Almighty Creator.

White

"Coming now to the white colour in the flag, this colour traditionally symbolises peace and here also marks the coming of Christianity which brought with it faith and purity. This colour will carry into the heart and soul of our people its message of peace and goodwill unto all people, symbolising the end of tribal wars and feuds, the termination of the struggle, strife and turmoil of the olden days and announcing the breaking of a new day, the advent of a new regime, the birth of a Xhosa-speaking nation and predicting that the 'eyes of the future are white'—that is, the future forecasts peace.

"The roots of Christianity have grown deep into the heart of our people and brought with it true peace of heart, and a thirst and hunger for improvement.

Green

"The green in the flag symbolises the beautiful green fields of the Transkei—the green of our hills, our valleys, our forests is exquisite and is nowhere surpassed in Southern Africa.

"No matter what we do to earn a living—whether we be attorneys, teachers, peasants or whether we delve in the bowels of the earth in search of its hidden treasures—there is one characteristic which is common to us all: we are all sons of the soil, children of the open veld, and although our daily tasks prevent many of us from enjoying the carefree life of the open veld which was the privilege of our forebears, it is apparent that deep down in our hearts there will always be that urge, that impelling longing for the wide open spaces of our green fields and it is therefore correct that green should be included in the flag, as indeed it is."

2

the case for independence

Many South Africans—and most foreigners—will be surprised to hear that the people of the Transkei do not consist of one individual nation in the true sense of the word. In actual fact, the Transkei consists of about twelve tribes. These tribes do not form a cultural unit but belong to two different ethnic groups—the Cape Nguni and the South Sotho, each in turn comprising a number of sub-groups. The name Xhosa refers only to a sub-group of the Cape Nguni. The Xhosa (Amaxosa) were originally known as the Aba-nguni, after an early ruler named Mnguni, of whom virtually nothing is known. A successor of his, at some later date, was known as Xhosa, from whom the tribe has taken its common designation.

According to J H Soga, the tribe probably originated in East Africa, being divided into a number of clans. They probably moved southwards from the area around Lake Victoria. In order to understand the later clashes between Blacks and Whites in the Eastern Cape, the following should be borne in mind: the Whites (Dutch settlers under the leadership of Jan van Riebeeck) landed in Cape Town in 1652 and this stream of Dutch settlers gradually expanded to the east. For more than a century these Whites did not encounter any of the Black people who were moving in the opposite direction, towards them. Only in about 1770 did these two groups meet in the area which is now around the present East London.

The Xhosas arrived in the Transkei before the year 1700, moving southwards. In 1686, survivors of the ship, the Stavenisse, encountered the Xhosas in the present Ngqeleni district. The first major encounters between Blacks and Whites increasingly led to clashes—altogether nine Frontier Wars. The struggle was further complicated by internal clashes between the Whites as well as between the Blacks.

The second British occupation of the Cape in 1806 was the cause of the tension amongst the Whites. After the arrival of the British Settlers in 1820, most of whom settled in the Eastern Cape, it became more and more difficult for the Dutch population and the British Settlers to pull together. This conflict led to the Great Trek in 1837-38, when most of the Dutch-speaking Whites in the Eastern Province trekked northwards. (Rapid occupation of the South African interior was brought about by the Great Trek which also led to many fresh encounters between Blacks and Whites.)

In order to understand the division amongst the Blacks, the abovementioned twelve tribes of the Transkei should be reviewed. The original Cape Nguni, who have lived in the area since the second half of the sixteenth century, are composed of:

Xhosa	Tembu
Mpondo	Mpondomise
Xesibe	Bomvana

Later arrivals who, as a result of the wars in Natal, streamed into the Transkei from 1825 onwards are:

Fingo (Amamfengu)
Hlangwini
Bhaca and Wushe.

The Xhosa consist of the Gcaleka, Rarabe (also known as the Ngquka or Gaika) and other tribes which cannot be classified under these two, and the Gqunikhwebe who are not related to the Xhosa but have been closely associated with them since the time of their origin.

In about 1702, owing to a series of quarrels, there was large-scale emmigration of the Xhosa across the Kei River, and a group led by Gwali trekked westwards. The main tribe under Phalo originally settled in the present Butterworth district. Phalo was the father of Gcaleka and Rarabe. The principal division of the Xhosa tribe took place between these two leaders. Rarabe, as well as Gcaleka, trekked into the present Ciskei. Eventually, after the Frontier Wars against the Cape Colony, the Gcaleka tribe settled in the district of Willowvale. After the Ninth Frontier War of 1877-78, other Xhosa from the Ciskei settled in the districts of Kentani and Idutywa.

My own tribe, the Tembu, is one of the largest in the Transkei. The Tembu, consisting of pure Tembu and naturalised Tembu, trekked into the Transkei towards the end of the sixteenth century and eventually settled in present-day Tembuland. The Qwathi and the Vundla joined us, the Tembu, here in the beginning of the nineteenth century. In 1828 the Ngwane, who were forced by Shaka to flee from Natal, invaded Tembuland. The attack was repulsed but resulted in part of the Tembu fleeing in the direction of Queenstown. These Tembu, known as Emigrant Tembu, formed a second group. In the Sixth, Seventh and Eighth Frontier Wars, the Emigrant Tembu joined forces with the Xhosa.

Following the defeat of the Xhosa, the Glen Gray district was set aside for the Emigrant Tembu, although in 1965 the districts of Xalanga and St Marks were offered in exchange for Glen Grey. However, only a section of the population moved to these two districts, so that the tribe ultimately acquired Glen Grey as well as Xalanga and St Marks. Ndala, the great-grandfather of our, the Tembu people, had fraternal relations with the Xhosa. He married a daughter of the Xhosas, namely the daughter of Hlaba. We then had a royal family of the Tembu. Tembu was the Chief of our tribe. Our tribe split in 1865. That is when my great-grandfather, Matanzima, the son of Umtitara, became independent and came from Lady Frere in the Glen Grey district to settle in that part of the country known as Emigrant Tembuland, with its headquarters in

Cala. This Chieftainship has been hereditary ever since. (Matanzima is only a name; Mata means spit (saliva); zima means 'have it'—have the saliva).

Tembuland stretched as far as the Katberg; the other side of the Katberg was inhabited by the Xhosa, that is the Calabe tribe. All of Queenstown was Tembuland, but the White people took possession of it after the skirmishes which took place between themselves and a Chief called Mapassa who occupied the area of Queenstown. The Great House of our family is in the Umtata district. Sabatha Dalinyebo is the Paramount Chief of the Tembu.

The following is a short summary of the history of the other tribes:

Mpondo

They seized Pondoland East before the end of the sixteenth century. In about 1945 the Mpondo tribe was divided between the two sons of Chief Fako (1780-1867), one group following Mqikela of the main house, and the other following Ndamese of the right-hand house. This division is still in evidence today with Botha Sigcau, a descendant of Mqikela, as Chief of the East Pondo, and Tutor Ndamase of the West Pondo. The Mpondo are settled mainly in Pondoland East (the districts of Lusikisiki, Flagstaff, Tabankulu and Bizana) and Pondoland West (the districts of Port St Johns, Ngqleni and Libode).

The Mpondomise

The Mpondomise, who are related to the Mpondo and Xesibe tribes, settled in their present territory (the districts of Tsolo and Qumbu) after having initially lived along the Umtamvuna River. In 1879 their territory was annexed as part of East Griqualand.

The Xesibe

This tribe has occupied its present history (the Mount Ayliff district) for many generations, repeatedly defending it against attacks by the Mpondo.

The Bomvana

They lived in Pondoland for about four generations, from where they moved to the district of Elliotdale (Bomvanaland), an area evacuated by the Xhosa.

The Fingo and other tribes were driven out of Natal by the Zulus. In the Transkei they are known as the Amafengu (people seeking a dwelling place). Initially, the Fingo established themselves mainly among the Gcaleka. In 1865 some 40 000 Fingo resettled in the territory between the Kei and Bashee Rivers, this area having been evacuated by the Xhosa.

The Hlangwini, Bhaca and **Wushe** belong to the fugitive tribes who seized no man's land after 1830. The Hlangwini live mainly in the districts of Umzimkulu and Matatiele, but there are also a number of them in the Willowvale district. The Bhaca are found in the districts of Umzimkulu and Mount Frere, and the Wushe mainly in the Umzimkulu district.

The **South Sotho** of the Transkei consist of the Kwena, Tlôkwa, Hlakwana and Rolong. The Kwena originally came from Lesotho, the first group having moved into the Transkei as early as 1859. The Tlôkwa originally came from the Harrismith area in the Eastern Free State. As a result of a clash with Moshesh, they moved to Herschel under the leadership of Sekonyela, from where a section of the tribe trekked to East Griqualand with Adam Kok and eventually settled in the Mount Fletcher district. The Hlakwana also hailed from Lesotho, and the Rolong came from Thaba'Nchu.

The **Sotho** of the Transkei are found mainly in the districts of Matatiele and Mount Fletcher, with small groups in the districts of Tabankulu and Qumbu.

From the above it will be clear that we do not all stem from the original Xhosa. We merely speak the Xhosa language. In the Transkei there are only three districts now that are inhabited by the original Xhosas. It is the Xhosa language that binds us together. The Xhosa language was the first to be developed as a written language in the Transkei and used as a medium of instruction in schools. In this way it has supplanted other Cape Nguni dialects and all the Cape Nguni tribes now speak Xhosa except for slight dialectic variations.

Before moving on to a discussion of the political development in the Transkei in the last century and the early part of this century, I also want to refer to one of the great calamities in the history of the Xhosas, a disaster that became known as the "Cattle Killing Delusion". In 1956 a young Xhosa woman named Nongquase, prophesied that if the Xhosa killed all their cattle and burned their crops, the Whites would be driven into the sea. Over 200 000 head of livestock were slaughtered, but nothing at all occurred on February 18, 1857, the date on which the miracle was supposed to take place. Starvation followed and it was officially established that the population of British Kaffraria dropped from 104 721 to 37 229 between January 1, 1857 and July 31, 1857. As a result of this disaster, and also, to some extent, because after the Eighth Frontier War the remnants of the scattered migrants took refuge in Willowvale and Kentani, the area south-west of the Kei became depopulated in 1862.

Taking these historical facts of the Transkei into consideration—and in view of our coming independence—it is necessary to bear in mind how the march to independence has been conducted by all the forces that were at work in its process of constitutional development. The Transkei received its name in the 1880s, which makes it older than the Union of South Africa which was only formed in 1910.

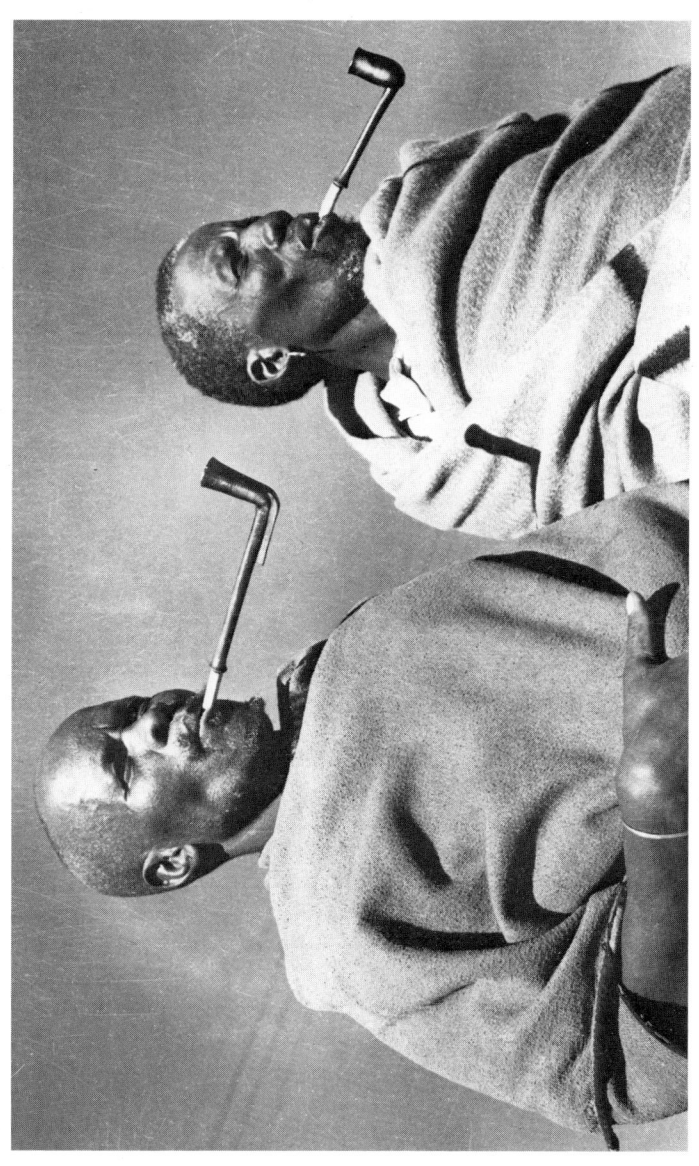

Men with their traditional long-stemmed pipes

It will, therefore, be appreciated why the Transkeians resent any suggestion that their country is a creation of the South African Government for the furtherance of its policy of apartheid.

Up to the middle of the last century, the people of the Transkei lived in totally independent Chiefdoms with their own legal system language and social organisation in the area between the Kei and Mtamvuna Rivers, between Lesotho and the south-eastern coast of Africa bordering the Indian Ocean. This independence was enjoyed despite the arrival of the White people in South Africa in 1652. In 1835 Governor Sir Benjamin D'Urban set up the "Province of Queen Adelaide" as a buffer territory between the Blacks and the Whites but received orders from London in the same year to return it to the Xhosas. It comprised the region between the old frontier up to the Kei River, between the Stormberg and the ocean. In 1854 Sir George Grey, Governor of the Cape and High Commissioner, urged that the area between the Kei and Mtamvuna Rivers should be brought under British rule. Nothing came of it, and the Colonial Government recognised the Transkei people as independent and able to rule themselves.

It was only after the granting of responsible government to the Cape Colony by the British in 1872 that the latter took positive steps to bring the Transkei under British rule by a process of annexations which covered the period 1872 right up to 1894. Europeans, almost entirely of British origin, then started settling in the Transkei in large numbers. It is important to know that the annexation of the Transkei was made subject to the laws in force in the Transkei. The people of the Transkei did not abandon their legal system and up to the present day Xhosa law is practised in the Transkei courts which are run on modern lines.

I should also like to point out that in terms of Section two of Act 38 of 1877 (Cape) providing for the annexation of the Transkei, no Act passed by the Parliament of the Cape Colony would extend, or be deemed to extend, to the Transkeian territories unless such act were extended thereto in express words. (The power of a Cape Governor to extend Cape statutes to the Transkei was inherited by the Governor-General of the Union in terms of Section 16 of the South Africa Act, which enabled him to extend a Union Government Statute to the Transkei by proclamation.)

Having completed the annexation, the British-Cape Colonial Government passed Proclamation No 109 of 1894 providing that no native may enter the Transkei without a pass. A native was defined as "any Basotho, Arab, Asiatic, Indian, Bechuana, Zulu and any aboriginal native of Central or South Africa." (However, history took its own course and at the 1974 Congress of the ruling Transkei National Independence Party some delegates spoke in the Sotho language, others in the Zulu language and others in the predominant Xhosa and English languages. Also, since 1964 one of the Cabinet Ministers of the Transkei has been a Sotho-speaking Chief, and there are thousands of Coloured people of mixed blood.)

A few more words on the Glen Grey Act (Act 25 of 1894). This Act made provision for eight location councils and a district council, and led to the creation of the Transkei Bunga. The district council consisted of twelve members, six of whom were appointed by the location councils and six nominated by the magistrate. The authority of these councils was confined to Glen Grey. This system, being purely Western-orientated, did not recognise the traditional administrative system of the Xhosa. Proclamation 293 of 1896 placed the Transkei under the jurisdiction of one magistrate.

Proclamation 352 of 1894 provided for the implementation of the Glen Grey Act in the Transkeian districts of Butterworth, Nqamakwe, Tsomo and Idutywa. This proclamation also abolished the location councils and established the Transkeian General Council, the Bunga, amalgamating the four district councils. A district council consisted of six members, of whom two were appointed by the Governor-General and four were nominated or elected by the inhabitants of the district. These councils met quarterly and the Transkeian General Council annually. In 1898 Kentani was included in the council, and in 1903 the system was extended to include the districts of Umtata, Mqnaduli, Engcobo, Tsolo, Qumbu, Mount Frere, Mount Fletcher and Umzimkulu. The Transkeian General District Council replaced the Transkeian General Council. In the same year, Willowvale was admitted to the new council, and was followed by Mount Ayliff (1908), St Marks (1909) and Matatiele (1911).

At this stage I would like to interrupt the political development of the Transkei, and pause for a while at the year 1910. In that year the British colonies (Cape and Natal) and the old Boer Republics (Transvaal and the Orange Free State) decided to form the Union of South Africa which later became the Republic of South Africa. Rhodesia was asked to join this Union but it refused. Swaziland and Basutoland (later Lesotho) which had previously been annexed by the Transvaal Boer Republic and the Cape Colony respectively, became British Protectorates and have since obtained their independence over the last ten years.

These countries, which are today members of the United Nations and the Organisation of African Unity, are no less South African countries than the Transkei is, bearing in mind that they share long borders with South Africa, belong to the same Customs Union with South Africa, and are land-locked whereas the Transkei is a coastal state. The Transkei, however, was by accident of history handed over to this Union of South Africa by the Cape Colony. The people of the Transkei were never consulted either about the formation of the Union or about their being handed over to it for administrative purposes. Its people accordingly became subject to segregation and discriminatory practices. The Transkei, however, never became integrated in the legal system of the Union of South Africa. The Union Government received the powers of the Cape Colonial Government as they were exercised over the Transkei.

I referred to some of these powers earlier on. In the sphere of Public Law, what are common law offences in the Republic of South Africa are statutory crimes in the Transkei based on a penal code which has no parallel in the Republic of South Africa. This code applies to everyone in the Transkei, irrespective of colour. It dates back to the time of the Cape Colonial Administration of the Transkei and is based on English law. (For example, as recently as 1974 the Appellate Division of the RSA reiterated that the law relating to murder and culpable homicide in the Transkei and the RSA has always been and still is different. The South African system is, of course, based on Roman-Dutch law.)

The road to independence taken by the Transkei, and my personal contribution in this respect to which I will later on refer in greater detail, is a process of orderly constitutional development such as was experienced by numerous countries in the world which are today independent. There was first the United Transkeian Territories General Council which met once a year and dealt with local government on a small scale. It was established on January 1, 1931, replacing the Transkeian General District Council and the Pondoland District Council. A standing executive committee was established in 1931. The Council had wider powers than the councils under the Glen Grey system and could promulgate regulations in the economic, industrial and social spheres. In 1956 the UTTGC was replaced by the Transkei Territorial Authority which had wide powers. This body came into being after the Bantu Authorities Act (Act 68 of 1951) and was made applicable to the Transkei in terms of Proclamation 180 of 1956.

Thus a start was made in establishing tribal, district and regional authorities and a territorial authority, after which the functions of the United General District Council and the district councils from which it had been composed were transferred to the new authority. The ultimate authority structure comprised a territorial authority, nine regional authorities, 26 district authorities and 129 tribal authorities. (District authorities were later abolished.)

The transition of power from the UTTGC to the TTA took place gradually, thus enabling the Blacks to make their own decisions as to where and how the new authorities were to be instituted. The aim of the Bantu Authorities System was to afford the Bantu an opportunity of developing their administrative skills to the stage where they would be able to run their own affairs. But over 20 White magistrates, appointees of the South African Government, sat in the House in an advisory capacity to the 120 odd Black Councillors. Each year it submitted numerous motions to the Government, covering matters of health, education, posts and telegraphs, etc., in the Transkei.

The Promotion of Bantu Self-Government Act, passed in 1959, provided for the development of self-governing Bantu national units, the so-called Homelands, and for the appointment of a Commissioner-General for each unit to form a link between the Bantu and the Central Government of South Africa. The desire for transition from self-government to complete sovereignty was first expressed in the Transkeian Territorial Authority when a motion calling for the granting of self-government to the Transkei was being discussed in 1961. Paramount Chief Sabata Dalindyebo, an elder brother of mine in the Tembu Royal hierarchy and head of the numerically strong Dalindyebo region of the then Territorial Authority, spoke strongly for the motion and declared amidst great applause:

I do not know why it has been suggested that we take time over the matter. I think that the Transkei alone has over 200 graduates. It may be surprising to know that there are countries in Africa where independence has been granted, but you can hardly find more than 20 graduates in these areas ... Some people are now eager to know what date independence should be declared. I tell them, it should be the date when this motion was introduced, that is, 19 April, 1961. (It will be observed that this motion was introduced when South Africa left the British Commonwealth. It is self-evident that the Transkei's colonial background entitles it to Commonwealth membership and it may well exercise its right to apply for such membership on attainment of independence.)

In that same year (1961) the Territorial Authority appointed a committee, made up of headmen and councillors, to investigate the implications of self-government. The negotiations that followed between the leaders of the Transkei and the South African Government resulted in the promulgation of the Transkei Constitution Act of 1963 (Act 48 of 1963) in which provision was made for self-government. On May 30, 1963, the Transkei was granted partial self-government.

Subsequently the Transkeian Territorial Authority was replaced by a partly elected Legislative Assembly which ushered in the period of "representative" self-government. District councils were abolished by the Transkeian Act 4 of 1965. At present, according to Section Nine (Act 48 of 1963), the executive authority of the Transkei is vested in a cabinet consisting of a Chief Minister and five Ministers (increased to six in 1973). In effect, as from 1964 the Transkei has been self-governing and has full jurisdiction over its departments of the Chief Minister and Finance, of Education, Roads and Works, Agriculture and Forestry, Justice, Interior and, as from 1973, Health. The Transkei Legislative Assembly makes laws which, however, have to be assented to by the State President of the Republic of South Africa before becoming legal.

The question of independence cropped up from time to time in the Legislative Assembly during the years 1964 to 1968. In 1965 a motion of the Transkei Freedom Party, calling upon the South Africa Government to grant independence forthwith, was defeated in the House. It was felt that a period of two years of self-government was rather short, and there were certain land claims which were being pursued by the ruling Transkei National Independence Party as a matter of urgency. The most contentious area was Port St Johns, whose beauty as a holiday resort is renowned. It, together with other areas, had been declared "White areas" on the granting of self-government in 1963.

In 1968 the Transkei Legislative Assembly passed a resolution asking the South African Government to do everything in its power to prepare the Transkei for full independence within the shortest possible time. (It should be borne in mind that the Transkei Constitution Act (No 48 of 1963) was passed by the South African Parliament following an announcement by the Prime Minister that the Government would be prepared to accede to a request for self-government for the Transkei.) In 1972 a firm request for independence for the Transkei was debated in the Assembly and in 1974 the motion in favour of independence was passed by an overwhelming majority. In the meantime the South African Government had agreed to transfer the "White area" of Port St Johns to the Transkei.

The Transkei is scheduled to attain independence on October 26, 1976.

Regarding the history of the Transkei as sketched above —my personal role in this respect will be reflected in more detail in later chapters—I would like to comment on certain aspects of it at this stage. Despite the fact that throughout the world in general, and Africa in particular, the people's thirst for freedom has always been acknowledged and encouraged, strangely enough a controversy has blazed up about the question of the Transkei's independence. A great deal of confusion has been sown and capital readily made out of the fact that the independence is being obtained from South Africa. It has been argued that this is "a grand design" by South Africa to perpetuate its apartheid policy. In fact, the Transkei's impending independence has been condemned outright on facts that apply not against it but against South Africa. The inescapable truth is that the policy of apartheid is not the policy of the Transkei. What is more, I have clearly stated that all efforts will be directed at the building of a non-racial democracy.

Therefore, one might expect all sincere opponents of apartheid to applaud the Transkei leaders for this breakthrough. But in the world of today, people are able to argue that black is white.

Pondos gather to drink beer

I, and also some of the other leaders of the Transkei, are depicted by some as stooges of the South African Government, presumably because we have attained our independence through negotiation. If we Transkeians had used our spears and battle-axes to try and achieve exactly the same goal as we have in fact achieved, and killed some 30 odd Whites in the process, we would be the heroes of the day even if half the population of the Transkei had lost their lives in the process, and the coming independence of the Transkei would be embraced with extraordinary enthusiasm by all and sundry.

In the light of the Transkei's colonial background, similar to that of Lesotho, Swaziland and Botswana for instance, charges that the Transkei's independence is wrong because it violates the territorial integrity of present-day South Africa, are transparently hollow. But there is also an element of double standards in this charge. As recently as September 1975, Lesotho's representative at UNO spoke of land claims his country was making against South Africa. If those claims are to succeed, it would mean the excision of parts of South Africa and the inclusion thereof in Lesotho. Yet there was not a single voice that objected to the claims despite their threat to the territorial integrity of South Africa. Indeed, "territorial integrity" is not generally upheld as a bar to anybody gaining independence where circumstances permit. Zambia and Malawi were part of the Central African Federation but they broke away and established their own sovereign states. In 1920 the people of Southern Ireland attained their independence from the United Kingdom. Recently Bangladesh did likewise, and there was no international outcry. And this only after enormous bloodshed—whereas we have attained our present status peaceably.

After exhaustive consideration of all the aspects and circumstances, I cannot be persuaded that it will in any way benefit the people of the Transkei in particular and the people of South Africa in general if the Transkei does not attain its independence from South Africa on October 26,

1976. We, the leaders of the Transkei, have indicated that the implication of the independence sought is that we will be free to have diplomatic and economic ties and trade relations with whomsoever we choose.

The fundamental interests of the Transkei and the Republic of South Africa are closely intertwined and in many respects they overlap. It is our intention, therefore, to maintain a cordial relationship with South Africa and follow a policy of good neighbourliness towards the Republic. Interference in internal affairs and dictates by South Africa will, of course, not be tolerated. To strengthen and formalise the existing good relations between an independent Transkei and South Africa, the two countries have already agreed on formal diplomatic ties and the exchange of diplomats at ambassadorial and other levels.

It is generally accepted that in today's world all countries are economically interdependent and the Transkei will be no exception. As I said in October, 1975: "My vision of economic viability for my country can no longer be regarded as a pipe dream."

This is because of the success of various economic projects embarked upon over the last ten years by the Transkei Government. Prominent among them are the tea plantations in the East Coastal region. There are also the irrigation schemes which hold promise of bringing about vastly increased maize and vegetable production. It is a reasonable expectation that by Independence the Transkei may well be able to defray current expenditure in the public sector without any help from the South African Government. This is predicted on the grounds that the Transkei has, from April 1975, been entitled not only to direct taxation of individuals but also to its share of sales, income and other taxes, as well as customs dues generated within its borders. As from independence, companies tax will also accrue to the Transkeian Revenue Fund. And capital works will require outside finance. Few third world countries can boast of such viability. To this end, application has already been made on the Transkei's behalf by the

Republican Government to the other members of the Southern African Customs Union (i.e. Botswana, Lesotho and Swaziland) for the Transkei's accession to the treaty. As is the case with the other members, the Transkei will remain within the Rand monetary bloc.

Industrialization is largely in the hands of the Transkei Development Corporation—a statutory body born of the defunct Xhosa Development Corporation which was specially created in 1965 to attract to the Transkei (and Ciskei) factories—particularly those of a labour-intensive type. Substantial monetary and fiscal inducements underpin this operation which is closely linked to the Transkei's ultimate economic viability and urbanisation. Urbanisation, in turn, is closely related to siphoning off surplus and unproductive rural dwellers and the much needed revision of agricultural land tenure to permit of larger scale farming. The main industrial activity centres on two growth points—Umtata and, to the south, Butterworth. Both centres are linked to the South African national power grid of the Electricity Supply Commission, national roads, railways, airways and the telephone network. Since 1965 more than 30 industries have been established there and a similar number of applicants are in the pipeline—particularly since my recent successful tours of the United Kingdom and the Continent.

The Transkei's Department of Defence will be formed at independence. Meanwhile the Republican Defence Force is equipping and training a Transkeian unit, initially of battalion strength and headquartered in an ultra-modern base eleven kilometres from the capital. The Transkei's defence policy will be quite independent of the Republic's but aggression by powers against the states of Central and Southern African will certainly be seen as a threat to Transkeian independence, to be combated in collaboration with sub-continental states with mutual interests. The Republic is clearly such a state and co-operation in defence matters is, therefore, to be expected.

The question has been raised as to what contribution, if

any, the Transkei's independence can make to the cause of freedom for the rest of the Blacks in South Africa. It has been charged that the Transkeians are wrong to seek independence because they leave their fellowmen in the lurch, and that the independence of the Transkei does not solve the problems of South Africa. It will be remembered, however, that the Kingdom of Lesotho, which is an enclave within the borders of South Africa, did not hesitate to take independence for its one and a quarter million people when the time was ripe, despite the fact that there are another one and a quarter million Sotho-speaking people living and working in South Africa, among the rest of the Black population of South Africa. Be that as it may, the Transkeians applaud the independence of Lesotho and of the 500 000 people of Swaziland and the 650 000 people of Botswana for the obvious reason that the number of Blacks under White rule was thereby reduced and the areas of freedom in Southern Africa accordingly increased. It is difficult to see why the independence of the two million people of the Transkei in an area exceeding that of Denmark cannot have the same effect.

When the time came, Southern Ireland became independent and Northern Ireland remained in the United Kingdom. What used to be Northern Rhodesia broke away from the Federation and became the independent Zambia of today. Malawi went its own way as well. Southern Rhodesia, as it was then called, stood alone—its Black population so to speak, left in the lurch by their breakaway brothers —if we have to accept this reasoning. No voice was raised against Zambia and Malawi, so we can dismiss the argument in the Transkei's case, too. The remarkable thing is not that Zambia "left them in the lurch" but that, having become independent, it was and is able to play an increasingly effective role in efforts to resolve the situation there.

In this regard I want to refer to a speech I made on October 16, 1975, when addressing a meeting at Flagstaff to explain the implications of the Transkei's forthcoming independence. I said at the time: "The Black people of Africa can never be entirely free until the Blacks of South Africa are free. The Transkei's independence will be a material contribution to that cause."

I have repeatedly expressed my belief in a Federation of States in this sub-continent of Africa. The independent Transkei would no doubt make a vital contribution to the political and economic interests of such a Federation. When considering the possible contribution of the Transkei's independence, it will of course be borne in mind that there is no magic formula for political problems. If there had been such a formula, the whole of Africa would have become independent simultaneously with Ghana nearly 20 years ago. In actual fact, the peoples of Africa have obtained their freedom at different times and in different ways.

3

my uphill battle for political rights

"That our road to sovereignty has passed through South Africa is something quite beyond our control ... and we call upon those who already enjoy freedom, particularly our brothers in Africa, not to visit the sins of the father upon the son ..."

With these words I ended my speech when I opened the conference of the Foreign Affairs Association in Umtata on April 20 this year (1976). On that occasion I spoke on the subject "The Transkei's Road to Independence", to which I will return later on. I am quoting from this speech in the meantime as, coupled with my views as set out in the previous chapter, my personal contribution to the constitutional progress of the Transkei will be seen in its right perspective in the following two chapters. In many ways it was a lonely road and not without a certain element of danger, but I did not hesitate to follow it as I had the interests of my people and my country at heart. I felt that this was my way of serving them ... and I am still doing this to the best of my ability. Therefore I am going to start this chapter with the year 1948, shortly after the Second World War, at a time when I had just completed my law articles and occupied myself with court work amongst my tribesmen in the St Marks District.

In that year the National Party, contrary to all predictions, won the General Election in South Africa. Just like Sir Winston Churchill, who led the British people during the war years only to make way for Mr Clement Atlee in 1945, Field Marshal J C Smuts was succeeded by Dr D F

Malan as Prime Minister of South Africa in 1948. The word 'apartheid' started to hit the headlines ...

This apartheid policy of the Nationalists was most attractive to me as an individual, although the majority of the African people did not approve of the policy of the National Party. But as far as I am concerned it appealed to me, because it came at a time when the Black people wanted to control their own affairs. It coincided with my desire to see my people free and with the passing of the Bantu Authorities Act in 1951, which made provision for the establishment of tribal, district and regional authorities and a territorial authority for the Homelands, I felt that this was the time for me to concentrate on working for my people.

As I have mentioned before, the United Transkeian Territories General Council was in existence since 1903, after the original council system was first established in 1895. This body continuously petitioned the Government for greater powers and in 1944 requested it to declare the Transkei "a Union Native Province or state with Sovereign rights in the administration and government of its affairs and people." This request was turned down as was one of 1946 that the Transkei become a fifth province of the (then) Union.

I became a member of the General Council again in 1954, after an interval of ten years, with the specific purpose of replacing the General Council with the Bantu Authorities System, and having this as the pattern for our future administration. We succeeded in this. In 1956 a resolution was passed in Umtata disestablishing the General Council and integrating the Council system into the Bantu Authorities system. A Recess Committee was appointed and I was a member of this committee. Although I wasn't the chairman, when it came to the tabling of the report I was nevertheless requested to table it.

I succeeded in getting the House to agree to all the provisions of this Recess Committee. This was known as the Transkeian Bantu Authorities Proclamation of 1956. In

The Bunga in Umtata

1959 Paramount Chief Botha Sigcau of the Pondo was elected as first chairman of this body, the Transkeian Territorial Authority (TTA). Thus a start was made in establishing the different authorities, after which the functions of the United General District Council and the district councils, from which it had been composed, were transferred to the new authority. The ultimate authority structure comprised a territorial authority, 26 district authorities and 129 tribal authorities. (District authorities were later abolished.)

A tribal authority is appointed to advise the chief or headman, with due regard to tribal laws and customs. His powers are limited to the affairs of the tribe or community over which he is appointed. A regional authority is composed of a number of tribal authorities of a region and consists of a chairman appointed by the State President of South Africa and a number of members elected from among the tribal authorities. The authority is empowered to advise the South African Government on matters of affecting the inhabitants of the area and is responsible for managing and establishing educational institutes, building roads, bridges, dams, combating soil erosion and stock diseases and building and maintaining hospitals and clinics. A territorial authority is elected from among the members of the regional authorities and liaises with the Commissioner-General for the ethnic group.

In 1961 Paramount Chief Botha Sigcau requested me to take over because of the trouble that we had in Eastern Pondoland, and I became the second chairman of the TTA. (In an enquiry Mr Justice Snyman found that the terrorist organisation Poqo was formed by certain extremist members of the Pan African Council (PAC) in 1961, and that it was the PAC which had gone underground. Acts of violence were directed against Whites and Chiefs. I was a particular target because I supported Government policies. From the end of 1962 members of Poqo from the Western Cape infiltrated into the Transkei with the object of taking reprisals against pro-government chiefs. Several attempts were made to assassinate me, and at least two headmen were killed. In several areas there was fighting between police and bands of Poqo members. On February 2, 1963, five Whites, including a woman and two young girls, were murdered at a road camp near the Bashee River in the Transkei.)

It was under my chairmanship that the TTA unanimously passed a resolution in 1961 requesting the State President to declare the Transkeian Territory as a self-governing territory in terms of the Promotion of the Bantu Self-Governing Act of 1959. A proposal was also accepted by the TTA that a Recess Committee be appointed "to go into the implications of the granting or otherwise of self-government to this Authority". I was chairman of this committee as well.

The proposal further charged the committee with considering:

a) the financial implications of the granting of self-government and the different kinds of taxation paid by the Transkeian population;
b) that self-government should in no way tamper with the chieftainship system;
c) the relations between the South African Government and the proposed state;
d) the possible date of granting self-government; and
e) the manner of approaching the South African Government to effect self-government.

The report of the Recess Committee was approved by the TTA in 1962 and after successful negotiations with the South African Government the Transkei was granted self-government in terms of the Transkei Constitution Act 1963 (Act No. 48/1963).

Thus we were the first Black people to request the Republican Government to apply the Promotion of Bantu Self-Governing Act of 1959 to us. On May 30, 1963, the Transkei was granted partial self-government. Subsequently the Transkeian Territorial Authority was replaced by a partly elected Legislative Assembly which ushered in the period of "representative" government. Many people alleged that this was imposed on the Transkeian people. This is completely wrong and intended to mislead the world. It is the Transkeian people, with their long history of administration, who made this request.

During the debates in the South African Parliament on the Transkei Constitution Act, the Opposition tried to make amendments, but Dr M D C de Wet Nel, the Minister of Bantu Administration and Development, very honest, said that it was a document which came from the Transkeian people and they wanted it as it was. At the last session of the Territorial Authority in December 1962, I tabled an unopposed motion of appreciation for the good offices of Dr de Wet Nel, who had piloted the Transkeian Constitution through Parliament without any noteworthy amendments. With the prospect of an election on November 20, 1963, the people of the Transkei became ever more conscious of the great developments in store for them.

But before we proceed to these interesting events, including my first test of strength against Paramount Chief Victor Poto of Pondoland, I wish to draw attention to the following message from the Executive Council of the Transkeian Territorial Authority to Dr H F Verwoerd, then Prime Minister of South Africa. It was handed to Dr de Wet Nel on the occasion of the Transkeian Union Festival celebrations in Umtata on April 6, 1960:

> "By means of this documentary message, the Bantu inhabitants of the Transkei wish to express gratitude for the help, assistance and guidance which they have received during the 50 years of the existence of Union. The good faith that prevails at present between the Government and the Bantu population of this area serves as proof thereof. It is our aim to build on the firm foundation which has been laid in various spheres during the first half-century of the existence of the Union of South Africa. We wish to declare through you to the Government and different sections

of the South African population that the Transkeian Bantu, during the following 50 years, will maintain and hand down to posterity their motto of 'loyalty to the Government'."

In this spirit I conducted all my dealings with the South African Government.

FIRST CONSTITUTION OF THE TRANSKEI

The Transkei Constitution Act (No 48 of 1963) conferred self-government on the Bantu resident in the Transkei and on certain Bantu related to the Bantu of the Transkei. The act is divided into ten different parts and deals, inter alia, with the Transkeian Territory, the Flag, the National Anthem and Official Languages, Citizenship, the Executive Authority, the Legislative Assembly, Chieftainship, the Judiciary, Finance and provisions regarding land.

Administration

It was decided that the Transkeian Government should initially have the following departments under its control:
> the Department of Education,
> the Department of Agriculture and Forestry;
> the Department of Justice (with control over the lower courts; high courts to be controlled by the present division of the Supreme Court for the Eastern Cape);
> the Department of Finance (to be managed by the Chief Minister);
> the Department of the Interior; and
> the Department of Roads and Works.

Citizenship

Transkeian citizenship was created for all Africans born (or who had lived for more than five years) in any of the Transkeian districts, all Xhosa-speaking Africans outside the Transkei and all Sotho-speaking Africans outside the Transkei who were members of tribes residing in the Transkei.

The Cabinet

The executive authority for the territory is vested in a Cabinet of five Ministers (increased to six in 1973) and a Chief Minister elected by secret ballot from among members of the Legislative Assembly. An important departure from the normal Western approach in the election of a Chief Minister is the provision that the Legislative Assembly must fulfil that function as a body. This was provided for in the Act at the request of the Recess Committee which wanted to ensure that confidence in that important post would be on a broader basis within the governing body; the committee also felt that it conformed more closely to the Bantu system of government.

The Legislative Assembly

The Legislative Assembly of 109 members consists of the five paramount chiefs of the Transkei, 59 chiefs elected by the chiefs on a district basis from among their own ranks; and 45 members elected by the voters of the Transkei. The number of chiefs and paramount chiefs may at no stage exceed 65. The 26 districts constitute the electoral divisions for the election of the 45 elected members. (In 1971 the number of elected chiefs was increased to 60, which implies that since then there have been 65 traditional figures of authority in the Legislative Assembly, which is unicameral. After Herschel and Glen Grey became part of the Transkei, the number of elected chiefs was increased to 69 and the elected members to 50, the number of traditional figures of authority thus rising to 74 members.)

In addition, several provisions in connection with the chieftainship were incorporated in the Constitution: inter alia, that the chiefs and the existing tribal authorities shall

Ex-President J J Fouché delivering the opening address to the Legislative Assembly in 1971

retain their present duties, powers and functions until such time as these are changed by their own legislative body. The reason for this, as was adduced during the discussions of the Recess Committee, is that Bantu concepts should not be disturbed and disrupted unnecessarily. The status of the paramount chiefs is protected within their own territories, while the ethnic-historic classification of the constituencies will also influence the composition of the Legislative Assembly during the election of its representatives. On ceremonial occasions, the personal status of the paramount chiefs enjoys precedence over all other persons within their own regions, even above the Chief Minister of the Transkei, provided that the occasion is not directly connected with the business of the Legislative Assembly.

Freedom of Speech

Section thirty-six of the Constitution provides for freedom of speech in the debates of the Assembly. No member of the Cabinet or of the Assembly will be liable to any legal proceedings by virtue of any matter which he may have brought by way of petition, draft law, resolution, motion or otherwise, or may have said before the Legislative Assembly. The public may attend the proceedings of the Legislative Assembly.

Justice

The Constitution provides for the transfer of inferior courts to the Transkeian Government of the creation of its own courts within its territory. The Attorney-General of the Eastern Cape Division of the High Court retains the right to refer cases from one court to another, irrespective of whether the case originated inside or outside the Transkei. The existing courts will continue to exist until their jurisdiction or composition has been changed by a competent authority. Section fifty provided for the institution by the State President, after the first Cabinet of the Transkei had been elected, of a high court for the Territory which would replace the existing divisions of the Supreme Court of South Africa, Bantu Appeal Courts and Divorce Courts in the Territory.

National Anthem, Flag and Language

The question of language rights of the Xhosa was discussed in the Republican Parliament early in 1963 when an amendment to the South Africa Act was discussed. The amendment which Parliament adopted recognised Xhosa as a third official language in the Homeland, next to English and Afrikaans.

The Commissioner-General

The title of Commissioner-General for the Xhosa national unit will be retained, and his functions will conform to the constitutional development. Up to the present it has been the task of the Commissioner-General to give guidance and advice to the Xhosa national unit. He has made it his duty to develop the judicature and law courts in the country. He also acts in close consultation with the people, particularly with the former Territorial Authority, the paramount chiefs, tribal chiefs, headmen and other representatives on all matters affecting the interests of the national unit concerned.

The Commissioner-General acts as a link between the Government and the Legislative Assembly. It is a function closely related to his former duty of enlightening the Transkeian people on Government policy and legislation, and of enlightening the Minister, in turn, on the needs and wishes of the people of the Transkei. Mr Hans Abraham, a former M P of the National Party for Groblersdal in the Parliament of the RSA, acted as Commissioner-General for the Transkei from July 1, 1960 to May 31, 1974, when he was succeeded by Mr D H Potgieter, a former Senator in the South African Parliament. In passing I may add that I regard both these gentlemen as my friends. I liked Mr Abraham, now retired and living in Pretoria, for his honesty and I have established a friendly relationship with the present Commissioner-General, Mr Potgieter.

OUR FIRST ELECTION: POTO VS MYSELF

The year 1963 was a year of great political activity in the Transkei. Small wonder, for on November 20 the Territory was launched on the next phase of its road to self-determination when the first general election in the Transkei took place. Shortly afterwards, on December 6, 1963, the members of the Legislative Council had to choose between Paramount Chief Victor Poto and myself. The first cabinet of the Transkei was also elected on that day.

The immediate task, however, was to get the people themselves to register as voters for the election on November 20, 1963. One and a half million registration cards had been despatched. In the Transkei the Bantu Affairs Commissioners had installed bureaux for registration purposes. About one million pamphlets had been disseminated in Xhosa and Sotho to tell prospective voters how, where and when to register.

As chairman of the former Territorial Authority I said in a radio broadcast at the time: "The people are inclined to overlook the fact that the Government of the Republic of South Africa has given the highest democratic right to the people of the Transkei, namely, to elect our own government. Both men and women over the age of 21 years can now vote, and if they are taxpayers they may vote even at the age of 18 years. For this we are grateful to the Republican government. But the gift we have received cannot be utilised if we do not fulfil our first duty, and that is to register as voters. As Chairman of the Transkeian Territorial Authority, I have been negotiating with the Government on this matter for the past two and a half years and I wish to appeal to every man and woman to report at their respective Bantu Affairs Commissioners and to register.

"Apparently there is a measure of uncertainty as to who are Transkeian citizens. If you were born in any district within the Transkei or have been residing there for the past five years or longer, then you can claim citizenship. This is also the case when your language is Xhosa or Sotho and your parents come from any of the districts of the Transkei. Even though you live on a White farm or within a White municipal area, but you originate from the Transkei, you can vote for the Transkeian Government which will be elected later this year."

According to preliminary surveys there were between 700 000 and 800 000 voters within the Transkei and the immediate vicinity; 95 000 in the Transvaal; 53 000 in Natal and 120 000 in the rest of the Cape Province. Some 13 000 voters, mainly Sotho-speaking, were in the Free State at the time. On June 17, 1963, some ten days after the start of the registration, the Commissioner-General for the Xhosa national unit, Mr Abraham, said that 200 166 Transkeian citizens had already registered. At the end of the registration period it was found that more than 90 per cent of the potential number of voters had registered, namely 880 425, of whom 610 000 were registered inside the Transkei and some 270 000 outside its borders.

The election campaign started with the nomination of candidates on October 2, and from the outset the election was dominated by the opposing viewpoints of Paramount Chief Victor Poto, who aspired to become the first Chief Minister of the Transkei, and myself. I advocated a Black Transkei with its own civil service, ultimate independence, exclusive African rights to land ownership, the franchise and participation in economic development, and with chiefs and elected members in a single chamber parliament. Mr Poto was in favour of the establishment of an Upper House of chiefs and an elected lower house, equal pay for all Africans throughout South Africa, and continued presence of Whites in the Transkei where they could have full citizenship rights. In brief, I accepted separate development and Mr Poto rejected it. I accepted the future

Transkei as an independent state; he rejected it.

All told there were 180 candidates with widely divergent policy statements, but the main attention was focussed on Mr Poto and myself.

On the eve of the election, I addressed large meetings in my electoral division. I was confident that candidates supporting me for the Chieftainship would be successful. But my opponents had been equally well organised. Throughout the election campaign Mr Poto enjoyed the support of Paramount Chief Sabata Dalinyebo of the Tembu. My own fortunes received an important stimulus when Paramount Chief Botha Sigcau of Eastern Pondoland declared himself in favour of separate development on November 11.

November 20—election day—dawned over scenes of great activity in the Transkei. From the Umzimkulu River in the north to the Kei River in the south, thousands of Black people made their way to the polling booths to elect the 45 members to the Territory's first Legislative Assembly. While some came by bus and on bicycles, many others arrived on foot. Elderly voters proudly rode to the booths on horseback. As I watched my people streaming to the polling booths, I thought with a certain amount of trepdiation: what does the future hold in store for them? And for me?

THE DIE IS CAST

Although local matters were also involved in the first General Election on November 20, 1963, most voters were aware that the main issue at stake was the election of the Transkei's first Chief Minister. It is especially noteworthy that the election went off without any untoward incidents. Although some of the candidates and their supporters exchanged a few harsh words, nothing interfered with the smooth course of events. I am convinced that much of the credit for this was due to the efficient manner in which the election was organised and the voters' obvious grasp of their new responsibilities. Although it was the first time in their lives that they had entered a polling booth, it was clear that many of the voters were well-versed in election procedures. This was due to the good work of officials of the Department of Information who had instructed voters in this matter over a period of several months. By midday on polling day it was clear that the percentage poll would be high considering the circumstances. Electoral officers estimated that the average poll would be at least 50 per cent.

The days immediately following the election were taken up with the colossal task of counting the votes. This was complicated by the large number of candidates and the fact that results in all parts of the Republic had to be telegraphed to the home constituencies. Shortly after polling day, the streets of Umtata began to resound to the hammers of builders, carpenters and other artisans who were modernising and enlarging the Bunga in order to accommodate the 109 members of the Legislative Assembly. They were doing everything possible to get things ship-shape for the first formal session of the Assembly on December 11.

It was clear that the people of the Transkei were entering a new phase in their history. Henceforward they would have to make every effort to secure efficient administration. They realised that there was still much to be learnt, and that they would have to proceed slowly and cautiously in the initial stages. Many also appreciated the fact that the South African Government, which had assisted them to reach their present position on the road to self-determination, would continue to extend a helping hand in the future.

The zeal with which the task had been tackled, the enthusiasm for the elections and the realisation of future responsibilities, were to me proof enough that South Africa's policy of emancipation without chaos had succeeded in its aim of creating a home for the Africans in their traditional areas in the Republic. I never was convinced that the climate was right for the resolving of these problems.

Commissioner-General Abraham stated after the elections that he was pleasantly surprised by the efficient manner in which the Black polling officials had acquitted themselves. He commented: *I believe that the African people will be able to assume full responsibilities for these duties in all future elections.*

Without political parties, the allegiance of elected members of the first Transkei Legislative Assembly was difficult to determine when that body assembled on December 6 in the historic Bunga building in Umtata. Prior to the long awaited election of the Chief Minister, the members of the Legislative Assembly were sworn in by Mr Justice A G Jennett. The seriousness of their demeanour showed that the members were deeply impressed by the dignified manner in which the wheels of the new machine of state were beginning to run. It became clear during the election of the Chairman of the Council that the struggle between Mr Poto and myself would overshadow everything else. The election of Mr N J Busakwe as first Chairman of the Assembly created the impression that Mr Poto would win, but when Mr Petrus Jozana was elected Vice-Chairman it was obvious that the choice of a Chief Minister was anything but a foregone conclusion. Commissioner-General Abraham got up and spoke briefly on the importance of these two offices. He then placed the robes of office around the shoulders of the Chairman and Vice-Chairman of the Assembly.

SYMBOL OF AUTHORITY

Mr C B Young, Secretary for Bantu Administration and Development, pointed out that most democratic countries used some type of mace or other to symbolise the authority and dignity of the Chairman of the Legislative Assembly. On behalf of the Government of South Africa he presented a beautiful mace to the Sergeant-at-Arms, Mr S Makatini. The tension was mounting when the Chairman called upon each member in turn to enter the polling booth and choose between the two candidates, Mr Poto and myself. The election was held behind closed doors but after the counting had begun the public were again admitted to their seats in the gallery. Shortly afterwards the Chairman announced the result of the voting: I had won by five votes!*

It was one of the greatest moments of my life.

On this historical occasion I rose and thanked my opponent for the excellent spirit in which the election had been conducted. I went on to say:

> "Today the world knows what Transkeians think about the future development of their Territory. They have given a clear and unambiguous verdict on the conflicting and irreconcilable policies of their two leaders. The people of the Transkei have unambiguously rejected the policy of multi-racialism in the polling booths. I give my people the assurance that I will tackle with the broadest vision the task of leading you to independence. It will, therefore, be necessary for myself and my supporters to strive for amicable relations between Bantu and Whites. This can only occur if the Whites grant the Bantu the right to share in the management of their own affairs in accordance with the policy of separate development."

I pointed out that I did not intend to make promises, but I gave the assurance that I would try to realise the policy of separating the Whites and the Blacks of the Transkei as soon as possible. I undertook to strive for a higher standard of living in the Transkei by creating more employment and increasing wages, and concluded:

> "The educational system of the Territory will enjoy the highest priority of my Cabinet and I have no doubt that we will do everything in our power to satisfy the wishes of our constituents."

More interesting events were to follow: the formation of my first Cabinet during the first meeting of the Legislative

---

*(It has generally been estimated that Mr Poto's faction won three out of every four seats. According to Carter's Information the result of the first election for Chief Minister in December, 1963 was as follows: Mr Matanzima received the votes of 42 chiefs and 12 elected members (54), against the votes of 16 chiefs and 33 elected members (49) in favour of Mr Poto. There were two spoilt papers—Publisher's Note.)

Assembly five days later, the emergence of my own political party and of the opposition party, and the ceremonial opening of the Assembly by the State President of the Republic, Mr C R Swart, in the following year.

4

emergence of two parties

Paramount Chief Victor Poto became leader of the Opposition and I formed my first Cabinet, comprising Messrs C K Madikezela, J Mosheshe, G Matanzima (my brother), B B Mdele and S Mvusi.

The year 1964 also saw the development of two political parties in the Transkei. The name of my own Transkei National Independence Party (TNIP) was made known on March 11, 1964 and a draft programme of principles was published. The TNIP's inaugural congress was held in Umtata on April 23, 1964. Paramount Chief Victor Poto's party, the Democratic Party, was formed on February 7, 1964. The Transkei People's Freedom Party, led by Mr Shadrack Sinaba, was short-lived.

A word on Mr Poto, since deceased: he was the most senior Paramount Chief in the Transkei. Since 1918 he had served on various local governing bodies in the Transkei, and from 1937 until 1945 he was a member of the Native Representative Council. At the time I am referring to, it was generally felt that he was acting on behalf of White economic interests. Our policies differed irreconcilably: my party subscribed to the policy of separate development, and his Democratic Party supports multi-racialism. When I formed my own party, I summarised its policy as follows:

"It is based on three principles: the acceptance of the concept of separate nationalities; that the Transkei is a nation in its own right; and that the Constitution makes provision for the fact that tribal Chiefs play an important role in legislation."

What was not known at the time of their formation, was the public support the parties could expect. The parties were functioning before the ceremonial opening of the Legislative Assembly by President Swart later in the year.

When the 109 members of the Assembly took their seats, my followers sat mostly to the right of the Chairman, and the members of the Poto Party to the left. The first clash came shortly after the opening. I moved that the Chairman be replaced. In the subsequent voting it came to light that I had the support of 63 members.

In passing I may mention that smaller parties were also formed, e.g. the Eastern Pondoland People's Party, the Transkei People's Freedom Party and the Transkei People's Democratic Party, but they never received much support. Over the years it was mainly a straight fight between my own Transkei National Independence Party and Mr Poto's Democratic Party.

Rules of Procedure

The rules of procedure in our Assembly are more or less the same as those in the South African Parliament. Bills, which are submitted by the Cabinet or private members, are read the customary three times. After a Bill has been approved by the Assembly, it is submitted to the Commissioner-General of the Xhosa people who, in turn, forwards it to the State President through the Minister of Bantu Administration and Development. Members may use any of these languages: English, Afrikaans, Xhosa and South Sotho.

State President's Speech

In his opening address the State President, Mr Swart, said that the Government of the Republic was considering certain aspects regarding the transfer of such land as yet not controlled or owned by the Transkeian Government. The State President gave the assurance that the Transkeian

Government could perform its duty towards its people and its country in the knowledge that the South African Government would continue to assist it. The technical knowledge and skill that South Africa had acquired during its own development would be at the disposal of the Transkeian Government.

My first Budget Speech

The first budget speech delivered by a Minister of Finance of South Africa's first self-governing Black Homeland was delivered by me in the Transkeian Legislative Assembly in June 1964. (I am Minister of Finance in addition to being Chief Minister.) I paid tribute to the Republican Government for the assistance rendered to the Transkei in the past, and emphasised the friendly relations which exist between our two governments. I made it clear that the Transkei was still part and parcel of South Africa and that the Territory regarded the Republic as its mother country to whom its people looked for guidance and assistance. A solid foundation for economic development had been laid in the Transkei on which to build a future for the Xhosa people. I said: "We are in duty bound to protect this heritage which was handed over to us and to develop the wealth of the Transkei for its sons and daughters."

Thus I started leading this country from 1963. My aspirations were that we must implement the terms of the Transkeian Constitution Act; that is how I got the Transkei lands transferred to the Transkeian Government from the Bantu Trust and also the zoning of the towns. A Development Reserve Fund was also established in 1964, and it started off with one million Rand. As the name of the Fund implied, its objects would be two-fold. Firstly, to finance schemes for the economic development of the Transkei and the exploitation of its natural resources and, secondly, to create a reserve from which to draw in lean years or from which to meet extraordinary expenditure which might be necessitated by national disasters such as floods, famine and drought.

I pointed out that a sound agricultural industry was vital to any country. As early as 1964 the Department of Agriculture and Forestry was providing a livelihood for about 10 000 people in the Transkei by way of employment. The granting of self-government to the Transkei in 1963 also created opportunities in many other spheres for Transkeians to serve their own community. That is especially true of our Public Service. Since the take-over of the administration by the Transkeian Government in 1963, the number of posts on the permanent duty sheet of the Civil Service increased by 500, and 10 000 positions were available for other employees such as labourers. On the whole the Republican Government had been most generous in its financial assistance and the people of the Transkei were grateful for the sound financial launching of the Transkei.

Consolidation of my Position in the Elections of 1968 and 1973

I took a bold stand in the second Election which took place on October 23, 1968. After five years of self-government, my party, the Transkei National Independence Party, accepted independence as an ultimate objective and made a request to the South African Government that the Transkei be prepared for independence as soon as possible. Various manifestoes were issued by the TNIP, the Democratic Party and the Transkei People's Freedom Party. There was a fair amount of consensus in respect of educational policy, improved health services, universal suffrage, the preservation of the chieftainship, etc. The manifestoes differed mainly on the acceptance or otherwise by the parties of ultimate independence for exclusively Black territories.

The TNIP stood for:

- Formal acceptance of the policy of the governing party in the Republic of South Africa: viz. separate political development of the various African territor-

Umtata's new skyline

ies and White South Africa with the goal of ultimately achieving independence;
- The gradual withdrawal of Transkeian Whites;
- Increased administrative and governmental responsibility;
- More land;
- Friendly relations with the Republican Government and the governments of the other self-governing or independent Homelands; and
- Conserving and fostering tribal laws and customs.

On the other hand the Democratic Party once again stressed its goal of a multi-racial South Africa of which the Transkei should form an integral part in all respects. In my election manifesto I pledged that the time was not distant when all Transkeian departments would be run by Africans and all districts in the Transkei would have Transkeian citizens as magistrates. I promised that my party would strive for independence, and pressed for the transfer of the departments of Transport, Health, Posts and Police from the RSA to the Transkeian Government. (At that time the Transkeian Government controlled only the departments of Chief Minister and Finance, Interior, Justice, Education, Roads and Works, and Agriculture and Forestry.) When this was achieved, I said, the Transkei would be virtially independent and its recognition as an independent state would be a matter of formality.

I made further pledges such as on the improvement of educational and agricultural facilities, the development of industries in the Transkei and a stand against Communism and terrorism. Among the achievements I listed the progressive replacing of seconded White officials by Africans, and the appointment of African magistrates to Transkei benches. The time was drawing near when all districts in the Transkei would have Transkei citizens as magistrates, as well as other judicial functionaries. This time the tables were turned. My Transkei National Independence Party won 28 seats against the Democratic Party's 14. Three

Independents were elected, of whom two rejoined the DP and one the TNIP. With the support of about 57 chiefs, I enjoyed an overwhelming majority in the Legislative Assembly.

1973 Election

In 1973 all the candidates of the Transkei National Independence Party issued a collective manifesto. The following is the complete text:

1. We pledge ourselves to give full support to the Cabinet in its efforts to develop the economy of the Transkei. We shall activate the Transkeian citizens in farming, building of roads and bridges, building of clinics, building of schools with Government subsidy, provision of water supplies for domestic and agricultural uses, compulsory education, commercial undertakings, irrigation schemes.
2. We pledge assistance to the Transkeian Government and its claims for additional land comprising the districts of Elliot, Maclear, Matatiele Farms, Mount Currie and Port St Johns.
3. We shall struggle, in support of the Government, to remove from the Statute Book all discriminatory laws which are a source of inhumanity, e.g. Pass Laws, Influx Control regulations, discrimination in wages and salaries, restriction of movement of stock.
4. We shall assist the Government to activate the establishment of industries in the Transkei so as to provide work for Transkeian citizens and augment the revenue of the country.
5. We shall press for the establishment of Farmers' Co-operatives, Land Bank and Trading Companies to step up the economy of the country.
6. We stand for complete independence and the federation of the Black states. Completely equality amongst all races is our objective.

My own manifesto endorsed in more general terms these objectives, as well as my belief that separate development would demonstrate to the world that Black and White in South Africa can live together. I also envisaged the building of a civilised society based on African traditions and customs.

The Democratic Party's statement to the press merely reiterated its rejection of separate development.

The results of the election on October 24, 1973 showed an even more remarkable swing towards my policies than had been the case in the 1968 election. In 1968 the TNIP won about 44 per cent of the votes, the DP about 36 per cent, the Independents about 18 per cent and the Transkei People's Freedom Party about 2,4 per cent. In the election of October 24, 1973 no less than 55,2 per cent of all votes went to the TNIP, the DP received only 26,9 per cent and the Independent candidates 17,9 per cent. The final result was: the governing party, the Transkei National Independence Party, won 25 seats and the Democratic Party 10 seats while eight independent candidates were elected. (Early in 1974, two members, one from each party, were elected in by-elections in Umzimkulu.)

On the eve of our independence I want to say this: we have passed several laws for our people for the improvement of their conditions and their standard of living. And not a single one of these laws was ever queried by the State President or sent back for reconsideration by the House, which proves that we have had a stable government since 1963. I consider the transfer of certain Government departments to the Transkei—as well as certain portions of land from the Republic to the Transkei to be the Transkei Legislative Assembly's most important decisions during its first seven years.

FULL INDEPENDENCE

Full independent status for the Transkei was requested by the Transkeian Government in a motion during the

Legislative Assembly's 1972 session—one year after Mr J J Fouché, the second State President to visit the Transkei, opened the fourth session of the second Legislative Assembly in April 1971. The request was made on condition that certain White areas be added to the Transkei: viz Elliot, Maclear, Mount Currie and the remaining White areas of the districts of Matatiele, Umzimkulu and Port St Johns. Early in March 1974 the Transkei National Independence Party's annual congress adopted a motion in favour of independence for the Transkei within five years, even without the land claimed by the Transkeian Government, on condition that independence would not prejudice the land claims.

It is interesting to know that the people who really want independence are the urban people. Motions to this effect were submitted to our Party Congress from Cape Town and Johannesburg. There is a notion that it is the tribesmen who press for independence; that we as a government are dragging the people to independence. This is not so; we have been encouraged in it by the people themselves—the townspeople. Therefore, on March 25, 1974 I introduced a similar motion in the Legislative Assembly. The opposition didn't oppose the principle of independence. They merely said that before we could consider this we should go back to the people so that they could cast their vote on independence. But we felt we should have our own system of referendum. My Government felt that this matter should be referred to the tribal authorities—to the tribal people to consider it and then pass a resolution after having discussed it, rather than go to a ballot box with the people not knowing what it is all about.

My Government also decided to consult the officially recognised bodies of the Transkei: The Teacher's Association, the legal fraternity, the Medical Association, the Women's Association, all the legitimate organisations that exist in the Transkei. All these people and organisations gave us an overwhelming mandate to proceed with the request for independence.

An independence committee, consisting of representatives of the Transkei and the South African Government, has for some time been preparing the territory for independence in October 1976. The work of this committee was considered by a joint Cabinet Committee. When independence is achieved the entire constitutional and administrative arrangement will, from the nature of the case, have to be changed in order to meet fully the requirements of an independent state. Before coming to the main provisions of the draft Transkei Independence Constitution, which was published on April 23, 1976, I want to refer to questions that are sometimes raised on what role the Opposition can play in an independent Transkei.

I want to reiterate that there will never be any clampdown on the Opposition in the Transkei. A general election will be held shortly before the Transkei achieves its independence. In the meantime five members representing the Western Pondos have defected to us and now support our stand on independence, and it is my conviction that there will be more defections from the Opposition benches, already reduced to only twelve members by March 1976. We would not like to end up with a one-party Parliament, but if the reduction in the Opposition's numbers continues they will become too small to act effectively and influence Parliament. This might well result in a more healthy situation. Party controls could be dropped and the chamber opened for free discussion. If the Transkei ends up as a one-party state, it will be for different reasons from those which have produced most of the one-party states in Africa. There will be no coersion at all, and members will be able to make up their own minds freely. Also, everyone seems agreed on the Transkeian Government's policy of non-racialism. I don't see what principles are left on which we Transkeian people still differ.

The main provisions of the draft Transkei Independence Constitution are as follows:

- The legislative power in the Transkei will be vested in

The Town Hall with the Government Building in the background

a Parliament, which will consist of a President and a National Assembly.
- The National Assembly will comprise the five paramount chiefs, 70 chiefs and 75 elected members. The National Assembly will meet at least once a year and will be elected for a period of five years.
- Transkeian citizens of 21 years old and over will have the vote and citizens of 18 years and over who are already taxpayers will also be entitled to vote.
- Only persons who are citizens of the Transkei and over 21 may be elected to the National Assembly.
- The President will be elected by the National Assembly and will have virtually the same power as the State President of South Africa. No one under the age of 30 may be elected to this office. A candidate must have been resident in the Transkei for at least five years. The President will hold office for seven years.
- The national anthem will remain *Nkosi Sikelel 'i Afrika*. The national flag will consist of three panels of ochre-red, white and green.
- The official language will be Xhosa, but Sotho, English and Afrikaans may also be used for legislative, judicial and administrative purposes.
- There will be 28 constituencies for the election of the National Assembly.
- The judicial power will be exercised by a supreme court, which will consist of a Chief Justice and as many other judges as the President may deem necessary.

Every person born in the Transkei will be entitled to citizenship, as will anyone born outside the Transkei but whose father is a citizen of the Transkei. Citizenship can be obtained by registration in the case of majors who are South African citizens. Any such person should, however, have been resident in the Transkei for at least five years.
- All the laws operating in the Transkei prior to independence will be maintained and will remain

effective, except in cases where they overlap the laws adopted by the Transkeian Parliament.

I should like to deal more fully, with the powers vested in the President. The executive power will be exercised by the President, who will act according to the advice of an Executive Council. The Executive Council will consist of the Ministers, who may not number more than 15. The President may, from time to time, create as many departments as he may deem necessary.

Other powers and duties of the President are, inter alia:

- The appointment of diplomatic representatives;
- The signing of international treaties and agreements;
- The power to declare war or peace, or to proclaim martial law;
- The arrangement of Parliamentary sessions and meetings.
- The President will be the Commander-in-Chief of the Defence Force.

Regarding the question of citizenship, it is the intension to form a Citizenship Board, consisting of three representatives each of the Transkeian and South African governments respectively, to decide on doubtful cases. A new chairman will be elected every year from one of the members, and each country will be given the opportunity to elect a Chairman from his own representatives. Meanwhile, it is with a touch of nostalgia that I think back to the last session of the Transkeian Legislative Assembly, which ended towards the end of May 1976 with a particularly moving rendition of *Nkosi Sikelel 'i Afrika*. It was a ringing farewell to the old era. Now we are looking forward eagerly to the new era of political independence and freedom from racial oppression. It was on this note that the 13-year-old Assembly closed down. When next it meets in the stately old Bunga in Umtata it will be a fledgling Parliament for the Republic of the Transkei.

The final session was dominated by the death throes of the traditional Opposition, the Democratic Party. The once powerful DP, whose founder, the late Paramount Chief Victor Poto of Western Pondoland, had come within a hair's breadth of beating me in the leadership stakes back in 1963, was in pitiful disarray. A few months before, the DP's leader, Mr Knowledge Guzana, had been ousted by the young accountant, Mr Henry Ncokazi. Then just before the session opened, Chief Poto's son, Paramount Chief Tutor Ndamase, defected to join my own party. As I have mentioned before, there are now only 12 members of the Assembly in the official Opposition after the rest of the Western Pondoland delegation followed their titular leader to the Government's benches. Mr Guzana then denounced Mr Ncokazi and formed the New Democratic Party (NDP) with six of his loyal supporters. With a majority of one on the Opposition benches, Mr Guzana regained recognition by the House as Leader of the Opposition. Two more members then left the old DP and sat as independents.

That is the way things are now, a stone's throw away from independence.

We will attain our independence at midnight on the night of October 25, 1976. There will be widespread celebrations, which will start on Saturday October 23, 1976 in the Transkei. But we have decided that in the Republican towns and in the districts of the Transkei, the celebrations should start on Friday 22. In Umtata the official independence celebrations are scheduled for Monday 25 and Tuesday 26.

On Independence Day I will look at our National Flag—at the red ochre which symbolises the unity of the people and ties with the soil that belonged to our forefathers, at the white which is a sign of peace, and at the green which symbolises the beautiful green fields of the Transkei—and I will realise that my long struggle for independence, my road to freedom, has come to an end. I trust that I will be able to set about the new task awaiting me—that is to develop our independent Transkei into a fully fledged state in the world gallery of nations—with the help of the Almighty.

5

blazing a trail for black recognition

"Transkeians have given Blacks new dignity by blazing the trail for recognition, and have persuaded Whites to think along more open lines in matters of race ..."

This was the gist of my speech when I opened a three-day symposium organised by the Foreign Affairs Association in Umtata on April 20, 1976. The symposium was attended by speakers and guests from America, Britain, France, West Germany, Israel, Taiwan and South Africa. Before proceeding, I might mention that one of the speakers, Professor Jack Spence, Head of the Political Science Department at the University of Leicester, England, had some kind things to say about the Homeland leaders in South Africa. Professor Spence said the emergence of a charismatic and energetic leadership in the Homelands had come as a surprise to many in Europe and North America. This well-known political scientist said it was once fashionable to be sceptical of this leadership. Continuing, he said: *Yet over the last few years there has been a dawning recognition among many analysts that Homeland leaders have acquired the capacity to play something of a creative role in the politics of Southern Africa.*

In my own speech, I touched more specifically on some of the subjects raised in the previous chapters, and in a following chapter I will return to these in greater detail as I think it is necessary that the world should know, once and for all, what my attitude is towards controversial national and international issues, such as terrorism. The following is the full text of my speech, entitled "The Transkei's Road to Sovereignty":

"The Transkei already meets three of the classic criteria for statehood: It has defined boundaries settled by a de facto population of some two million people and is ruled by a stable government which is in total and effective control. On 26 October it will meet the fourth criterion namely that of absolute sovereignty regarding its own affairs. Seen against these criteria there should be no problem as to its international position and the Transkei should be recognised by and absorbed into the international community without further ado.

"Unfortunately in a world where political movements and terrorist groups which do not meet any of the normal criteria for statehood are, for all practical purposes, accorded such recognition, the Transkei has been told, in advance, by the United Nations, the Organisation of African Unity and sundry others that international recognition is to be denied it. It remains to be seen whether, as I suspect, this opposition will crumble, but for the moment this is one of the obstacles in our future path.

"I will now trace the road the Transkei has followed (and is following) to sovereignty and also look at the reasons why we have chosen this path. Let us start at the beginning. Southern Africa, as was the case in many other parts of the world, was for hundreds of years the place where enterprising and aggressive Whites from Imperial Europe met, traded and fought with, and, finally, conquered and exploited Blacks from whom they were, and in many cases still are, separated by language, culture, a millenium of mechanical inventions as well as skin pigmentation. I am not here to recap all these conflicts or to apportion blame and I mention those far-off days solely as historical background to the theme I wish to develop. This theme is that the things which have, for so long, divided Black and White in the Republic are so fundamental, emotive and related to the existence of undeniable ethnic loyalties, dislikes and acquired fears that they simply cannot be glossed over in instant Republic-wide, multi-racialism, one-man-one-vote and majority rule which would do no more than paper over the cracks.

"Tracing events further, many of the subjugated Blacks became the hewers of wood and drawers of water on the farms and, later, in the mines and factories of the Whites. The labourers were tribesmen born and bred and, mostly, they stayed that way. Landless, ignorant and poverty-stricken, their offspring doomed to the same life, their manners crude to Western eyes, they occupied the very lowest rung in the social order. In the eyes of their White masters and employers Black skins became synonymous with much that was, and is, unacceptable in a civilised society. Thus it was that personal aversion reinforced enmity resulting from centuries-long armed conflict in a web of rejection of Blacks by Whites which, if we are realistic, persists to this day. It is no earthly good wishing this hard fact away! The array of apartheid legislation which regulates the South African way of life from cradle to grave is, therefore, based, if not on morally defensible criteria, then certainly on reasons which, to the vast majority of Whites, are pragmatically correct.

"So, Gentlemen, the Progressive Reformists and Liberals of this country and their sympathisers outside our borders are, I am afraid, on the wrong track. I do not for one moment doubt their very real concern. They realise that history is strewn with the wreckage of aristocracies which failed to share power and wealth with their serfs; they recognise basically the same situation in South Africa and they wish to end it partly out of altruism and partly, I suppose, to salvage what they can of the society they know. I have no quarrel with these good peoples' basic intention which is to ensure the maintenance of civilised standards whilst giving the Blacks, Coloureds and Indians a real stake in the national economy and body politics. But, inasmuch as their success depends on millions of Whites accepting, in short time, a set of values totally at variance with all they and their fore-fathers have ever known, it is all pure 'pie in the sky'. That being so, my Government, many years ago, faced squarely the question 'What are the alternatives?'

"I shall tell you what they are:

(a) We can accept that South Africa is immutable; or
(b) We can engage in bloody revolution in an attempt to bring about the collapse of what is to the Black man an unjust society, upon the rubble of which a new, just, multi-racial society—hopefully free of the old tensions—will arise; or
(c) We can try to achieve the same end without violence and bloodshed by working within the system.

"Acceptance of the *status quo* as permanent we—along with all other thinking South Africans—rejected out of hand. I do not intend even dignifying such a proposition by giving reasons. Revolutions along classical Marxist lines, the next alternative, is a concept relatively easy to 'sell' to those who have nothing to lose. In Africa it has proved appealing to an alarming extent. The vast disparity between the material welfare of the Whites and the Blacks has, everywhere, afforded the Communists all the evidence they have needed to convince backward peoples that all they have to do is to take up arms, kill the White man or chase him away, take over his prosperous farms, industries and way of life and their troubles will be over. We in the Transkei know poverty. But we also are not in the position of having nothing to lose. We have thousands of schools, many dams, irrigation schemes, roads, courts, administrative complexes, 32 000 government employees in a civil service which is 96 per cent Black, a stable Black government, considerable industries and more to come. The peasant life in a rural tribal situation is, moreover, a tranquil, even satisfying one. Cash incomes for tribesmen may be low but needs are simple and people are generally happy. The institution of chieftainship ensures an ordered society and, in our tribal ways, each person knows his or her place. It is an honourable way of life, which many an industrialised state can envy.

"My Government believes it should change gradually to meet the demands of the 20th century, but can see no virtue in mobilising these peaceful people into a revolutionary army bent on military confrontation with the Republic. *Firstly,* it would be militarily suicidal; *secondly,* it is quite unacceptable to us morally —we who have been dealt with violently so often in our past have no wish to deal violently with others, *lastly,* it is quite unnecessary—we are closing the wage gap dramatically and generally getting all we want without a shot being fired! In a nutshell, peaceful evolution has always been my Government's platform and so it shall remain.

"This brings me to the third alternative. In South Africa in 1963 and even today, the only evolution possible is within the framework of the policy of separate development laid down by the Republican Parliament in Cape Town. We opted for this alternative for reasons I will discuss shortly. Permit me to link this assertion to the foundation which I laid earlier in my speech concerning the rejection of the Black man by the White man.

Magwa waterfall

Dr Verwoerd

"The late Dr H F Verwoerd, during his lifetime and even after the target of so much vilification by South Africa's enemies, knew his people better than most. And by 'his people' I mean not only the Afrikaners but also the English-speaking Whites. Apart from a liberal fringe prepared to share their all with people of other colour, South African Whites were, twenty or so years ago, divided only on side-issues like Sunday sport, lotteries, mother-tongue education, etc., but were united in their attitude towards the Blacks. These were perceived, in essence, as non-persons, labour units, legal objects rather than legal subjects, assets in the national inventory, socially objectionable and to be kept out of skilled jobs, national sport, the armed forces and politics in perpetuity.

"This all-pervading rejection of the Black and Brown peoples took no account of the growing numbers of sophisticates among them—people of superior education who met all the requirements for social acceptability, job equality, etc. etc., but who simply could make no breakthrough in these fields in the rigid White-dominated society then extant. A Black doctor was seen as being no different to a Black streetsweeper and it was held by conservative Whites that any concession made to the Black doctor in regard to, for instance, accommodation at a White hotel, would inevitably result in the labourer and others at intervening levels also seeking concessions. This would in turn lead to the destruction of the White man's traditional way of life.

"In this stultifying atmosphere no progress in the emancipation of the Black and Brown peoples was possible. A political and social logjam dammed the mainstream of development in the Republic. Black consciousness and resentment grew in inverse proportion to the capacity of the White society to do anything positive about it. Dr Verwoerd took all this in and, in collaboration with far-sighted colleagues and advisers, came to the conclusion that pressures behind the logjam would eventually become irresistible and lead to catastrophe. Something had to be done to dismantle the dam bit by bit, gradually to release pressures and altimately to set the mainstream in motion again, and all without sinking river traffic or destroying property along the banks. It was a formidable engineering task.

Separate Development

"From this insight was born separate development. Not a perfect policy, to be sure, but the only one which could and can work in the Republic given all the complexities of the situation. It is not for me to go into details but the main objects of separate development, as seen by my Government, are:

"Firstly:
"To remove from Whites the fear that a better deal for Blacks in any field, particularly in politics and economics, threatens the existence of the Whites as a group which itself has fought for its rights many times before and has no intention of forfeiting them to a Black majority;
"Secondly:
"To create identifiable areas—not necessarily initially consolidated—where Blacks have political rights and can exercise them without running into White opposition based on the fear to which I have just referred;
"Thirdly:
"To develop these areas economically to stop the drift of young Blacks to those areas designated for White hegemony with the double benefit of restoring family life to Black workers and hopefully, ultimately,

of making possible the relaxation or scrapping of influx control.

"*Fourthly:*

"To create an atmosphere in which it is possible for Whites to accept the leaders of these new Black political entities as equals in the same way as Blacks from other parts of the world are when they enter White South Africa as distinguished visitors and make use of facilities hitherto reserved for Whites;

"*Lastly:*

"Flowing from the foregoing, to restore personal dignity to Black and Brown South Africans and gradually to condition Whites to the equality, in every way, of Black and Brown people who meet the requisite norms. In this way the social intercourse between the various population groups will, in time, assume a profile acceptable to all population groups here and, most importantly, to the rest of Africa and the world. Re-admission of White South Africans to the world society from which they are increasingly isolated and a prosperous contented Southern Africa is the prize.

"You will notice that I have gone out of my way to stress that this policy of separate development is a White man's policy. Its primary goal is unashamedly the preservation of a White identity and control by Whites over their own destiny. My Government respects the policy for this very honesty because we have, all along, believed that South Africa has *no* 'native' or 'Black' or 'Indian' or 'Coloured' problem —it has a White problem. It is the White group which has to come to terms—sometimes agonisingly —with a world that is overwhelmingly Black, Brown or Yellow! It is our duty to help them make the necessary adjustment.

"If separate development is the only way in which the vast majority of Whites in South Africa can be persuaded to allow their Black countrymen a better way of life, then my Government will do everything in its power to assist the Republican government—and, in particular, Mr John Vorster, who is handling with aplomb an extremely volatile situation—to make the policy work in so far as the Homelands are concerned. We must not precipitate a White backlash by immoderate demands and extremist posturing.

"That is why my Government believes it has been best for South Africa in general and the Transkei in particular to have accepted self-government in 1963 and to opt for independence in 1976. It has set the pattern for the granting of similar benefits to our Black brothers in the Homelands and our quiet progress has done much to allay White fears. When in 1963 I entered a White hotel, people stared. I probably ran some risk of being thrown out. Today they don't even bother to turn around to look. In 1963 a Black and two Brown South Africans attending the United Nations General Assembly as part of the Republic's delegation was sheer fantasy. In 1974 reality. In 1963 a Black athlete at the Pilditch Stadium in Pretoria was unthinkable. Today White and Black spectators there cheer a Black winner and clap sympathetically for a White loser. Black and White boxers belt each other before mixed audiences —and the heavens do not fall! The All Blacks (once all-White) included Maoris in their last two touring teams; the French tourists a Black and now, at last, mixed teams of South African rugby players and cricketers are taking the field. Call it multi-national if you like ... a rose by any other name ... but I put it to you: Do you think any of this would have been possible without separate development and without a Black Government—the Transkei's—having been courageous enough to have accepted the challenge as well as the initial opprobrium accorded to supposed 'White stooges'?

"Well, I will give you the answers to both questions:

Positively not! We would, like the Jews during the Diaspora, still have been despised as 'kaffirs'. Just as Jews everywhere gained a new stature with the coming into being of the Promised Land, Israel, so too we Transkeians have given all Blacks in South Africa new dignity by blazing the trail and founding a Black Transkei. And we have succeeded in getting ordinary South African Whites to start thinking along more open lines in matters of race; of this there is no possible doubt!

"I have now explained at some length how I see the policy of separate development, how my Government moved within this framework and what the advantages thereof were to both the Transkei and the Republic of South Africa. Since 1963 the Transkei has developed steadily and will on October 26, 1976 become politically sovereign.

I would like to give a short analysis of our expectation of the future as regards both problems and possibilities.

"Firstly:

"We expect recognition of our independence by the world, particularly by our brothers in the rest of Africa. Armed struggle, rivers of blood, genocide and resulting famine seem all too often to constitute the entry qualifications of today's community of nations. Where such a struggle and suffering was *necessary* for a people to secure freedom, let it be so and let the fighters be admired for their perseverance. But where freedom has been gained peacefully, who is to say it is less meritorious? If independence by negotiation be a disqualification for membership of the United Nations and the Organisation of African Unity then why are Botswana, Malawi, Lesotho, Swaziland, Zambia and Tanzania, to name but a few, honoured members? Their independence, like ours, came across a conference table and with the loss of no more than a few bottles of ink. No, we shall apply for membership

Xhosa woman with traditional long-stemmed pipe

of all relevant international bodies in the knowledge that our cause is just. If membership is denied to us it will represent a grave injustice toward a new nation more populous, larger in area, more advanced and more stable than many states who are already members.

"Secondly:

"The Transkei will enter into monetary and customs agreements with the Republic on the same basis as the ex-Protectorates. We expect in addition that the Republic will continue to assist us as it has done in the past. I have no doubt there will be people who will immediately point to both the agreements and the direct aid as being indicative of our economic dependence on the Republic. In answer to such accusations I can only point to the ex-Protectorates which likewise have such agreements with the RSA and to other African countries receiving aid from the Republic of South Africa. Even President Samora Machel (who receives payment of his mine labourer's wages at the *official* gold price) has, despite his revolutionary fervour, not seen his way clear to dispensing with this direct grant from the Republic of South Africa.

"Although the Transkei is by no means a rich country it is also not a destitute country and could make do without financial aid. But why should it refuse such aid if there are no strings attached to it? Certainly financial aid, no matter from whom it comes, benefits our development and the fact of its receipt in no way constitutes a disqualification for political independence.

"Thirdly:

"We expect that the example we will have set in terms of the foregoing will result in the amelioration of the lot of the Black people residing and working in the Republic. Remote citizenship has serious disadvantages in the opinion of my Government. It is our view that, apart from migratory workers, the millions of Blacks in 'White' South Africa are unlikely soon to return to the Homelands in significant numbers. Our ties of blood and citizenship with these people will not be broken but their interest in the domestic politics of an independent Transkei may be expected gradually to wane and increasingly to become comparable with that of, say, South African Jews in the affairs of Israel: benevolent concern and, in times of danger, even voluntary patriotism but divorced from the immediate aspirations, economic and civic, of the Jew in Johannesburg. We expect, in other words, that the Republican Government will not regard independence for the Transkei and, later, other Homelands, as the *last word on Blacks in general and Transkeians in particular in White South Africa. On the contrary, we expect White South Africans to make their lives at least as acceptable as those of foreigners of European extraction living and working in the Republic.*

"In summary then, Gentlemen, we will have in the Transkei after October 26, 1976 an independent state of multi-racial character with a free economy. It will be a sovereign state that will conduct its own affairs as it sees fit but which will have economic agreements and ties with other countries. We feel that this will benefit the Black man not only in the Transkei but also in the Republic. It will also benefit White South Africa. It will be a state with a free economy in which investment will be welcomed.

"I am satisfied that we shall fulfil our international obligations—if we are allowed to. If we are not accepted initially by the community of nations it will be because of the road to sovereignty which the Transkei has followed, namely orderly both through negotiations and peaceful progress within the framework of the policy of separate development. In that event, as I have often said before, we will be the victims of gross discrimination related to the fact that

Great Britain handed the Transkei on a plate to the Union of South Africa in 1910 instead of keeping it a protectorate. That our road to sovereignty has passed through South Africa is, in other words, something quite beyond our control and we call upon those who already enjoy freedom, particularly our brothers in Africa, not to visit the sins of the father upon the son."

6

terrorism, communism and other issues

During my long public career I was, for various reasons, questioned by many people on my views regarding certain issues such as apartheid, terrorism, Communism, capitalism ... the relationship between Whites and Blacks, economic interdependence, membership of international bodies, etc.

In a country with so many various national groups, a country on the southern tip of a vast Black continent, particularly high demands rest upon a Black leader to successfully separate chaff from wheat. At times one can only guess at the motive behind these questions in order to serve a specific purpose. One need only think about the wide division between Afrikaans- and English-speaking Whites who are traditionally composed of two parties, namely the National Party and the United Party. Since 1959 the Progressive Party, later joined by the Reformists, also became a political factor, and the Progressive-Reformists today enjoy the support of the powerful English Press in South Africa. Then there are also nine Black Homelands in South Africa in addition to large Black masses in cities such as Johannesburg, Cape Town, Durban, Port Elizabeth and Pretoria—people who are becoming more and more articulate in the political field and of whom many no longer have close ties with the countries of their origin.

Notwithstanding these factors, I have expressed my opinion at length on the issues of the day in speeches and interviews, which I summarise hereunder.

TERRORISM

I dealt with this topic in my policy speech on March 28, 1974 at the second session of the Third Assembly. After referring to some technical matters, I continued: "There are however, a few matters of a political nature which I would like to deal with briefly. The first and most important one is terrorism. I have on several occasions made it clear that my Government rejects the doctrine of Communism. We as a Government feel that South Africa's problems will not be solved through anarchy and other revolutionary methods as employed by the Communists, but rather through mature and balanced dialogue and negotiation.

"We prefer to remain cool-headed rather than succumb to emotional calls from irresponsible elements for throwing off the so-called yoke of White oppression. Emotions are not a very reliable agent for solving problems. On the other hand intellectual methods are. Our convictions are not based on our emotional response to cries for violence against those who have oppressed us but on the factual position existing today. There is no denying that there are certain aspects of the Republican Government's policy of separate development which annoy us. But, Mr Chairman, they are minor parts of the policy. The basis of the policy, viz. to assist the African peoples of South Africa to reach full independence (and here I am not referring to political independence only) is healthy and has opened up avenues for development which never existed before. Why, honourable members, shall we then elect to see only the negative side of the policy? Why shall we not grasp the opportunities under this policy to become absolutely free under circumstances which will guarantee future good relations between us and the other states of Southern Africa?

"And that, Mr Chairman, brings me to terrorism. The terrorists call themselves 'freedom fighters'. But who do they want to free? And if anybody is to be freed, why then by violent and revolutionary means? We are not bound by anybody! We can get political

Chief Minister K D Matanzima

independence any day we wish, and we get it by perfectly legal and constitutional means. All the machinery has been created to allow and enable each Black national unit in South Africa to develop as far as it wishes. Additional to the creation of the opportunities for development, the Republican Government had always signified its willingness in very positive terms to assist us financially in our quest for political and economic development. Provided, therefore, we are also prepared to do our share by working for the betterment of our own lot, there is really nothing which should deter us from realising our most elevated ideals without the aid of revolutionary methods.

"It should be clear, therefore, that these so-called freedom fighters have no part to play in freeing anybody in South Africa. What they are aiming at, therefore, is to create chaos to open the way for a wholesale takeover by their sponsors, the Communist countries. Let me assure you, Mr Chairman, these countries are not seeking the well-being of the Xhosas, Sothos, Vendas or Zulus. Because of its strategic significance in world politics, they are after the territory we occupy. Their aim is world domination, and to gain control of South Africa will assist them greatly in achieving this goal.

"We have no role or benefit, honourable members, in the aims of these terrorists. All we stand to gain by their actions is the eventual loss of our freedom, territory and identity; the loss also of what both Black and White have worked for for years in this country. That is why we are against terrorism as practised in Africa. And that is why we are against Communism and its satellite organisations—organisations which, although they are not purely Communistic, are assisting the aims of Communism. My Government, as a responsible Government, adopted an unshakeably strong standpoint against all terrorism. I feel the world should know that we, as a Black Government in South Africa, have no need for terrorist activities; that we feel that terrorist revolution will only break down everything we have achieved; that it will put us back decades in our development; and that every person or organisation assisting these terrorist organisations, either morally or materially, is committing a crime against the people of South Africa, be they Black or White. I hope, Mr Chairman, the world, and particularly those so-called liberation movements and everybody who supports them will take note of what I have said today."

I also referred to this burning question on other occasions. As far back as September 18, 1971, I appealed to the South African Government to allow members of the Black nations to share in the defence of South Africa. At the ceremonial installation of the first urban representative of the Transkeian Government in an African township in the Republic —at Tembisa between Pretoria and Johannesburg—I told the audience:

"We call on the Government of the Republic to enlist Black men in the Defence Force to help the White men against their common enemies who threaten to use force against this country."

Speaking at the celebrations held on December 11, 1973, at the Rotary Stadium in Umtata to mark the tenth anniversary of Transkei self-government, I warned:

"African states who encouraged the Arab oil boycott and were friends of terrorists should keep their hands off South Africa. It is most disturbing to find that there are still people who have no national consciousness, little political interest and have no realisation of their potential power or future destiny—people whose motives are to wreck what we have built over the past ten years. Such people would welcome the marauding forces of Communistic ideologies prominent in certain African countries that have encouraged the Arabs to boycott and strangle the economic and industrial development of South Africa by withholding their oil supplies. These people have also made a clarion call on America, Britain and European countries to stop supplying South Africa with any materials for its existence as a nation. The pretext was that these people would like to force social and political change in South Africa. I would like to warn these people, who are also friends of the terrorists that have destroyed Black lives in Rhodesia, to lay their hands off South Africa and examine their own position first."

When I welcomed the new Commissioner-General for the Xhosa National Unit, Mr D Potgieter, to the Transkei on June 6, 1974, I returned to this topic. I said inter alia:

"This is a stage when the relationship between the Transkei and South Africa should grow even closer because of the world situation. South Africa is our common home and we do not want the *status quo* disturbed by external revolutionary forces. The Transkei seeks the most harmonious relations with South Africa. Where we have to differ, let us differ as a family and not try to fight each other when we have common enemies outside South Africa."

When I opened the Xhosa Development Corporation's pavilion at the Rand Show on April 21, 1975, I said:

"Our development in the Transkei is following an orderly pattern and is securely underpinned by solid foundations which are capable of taking any stresses which may be placed upon them in years to come. This should to a large extent be attributed to our excellent relations with the Government of South Africa whose wise guidance, goodwill, co-operation, trust and material assistance have always been readily and generously available. The Transkei is justifiably proud that progress has taken place in an atmosphere of complete peace and tranquility on a continent where political, constitutional and socio-economic development has often been accompanied and marred by turmoil, conflict and revolution."

In conclusion I want to sum up: We cannot have a people seeking freedom whilst slaughtering one another. You will not find that in the Transkei. Our country will become independent peacefully and we are determined to live peacefully in our territory. Fortunately we are all related to one another in the Transkei, either by blood or marriage. This relationship makes the leaders—that is the hereditary leaders, the chiefs—united in everything we do.

This brings me to my convictions on other matters mentioned in the beginning of this chapter.

NATURAL CAPITALISTS

Firstly, the government and people of the Transkei are natural capitalists who place great store on their personal belongings. Not that we are materialists, to the exclusion of all other factors, but we, who are increasingly a part of a Western consumer society, value the fruits of labour. My Government's policy is one of capitalism with a conscience (the so-called mixed economy of the West). In the new Transkei there will be no equal division of profits. People are not equal; they deserve different compensations. Rather, there will be a just division. Those who use their initiative to reap higher productivity will earn more. There will be no talk of penalising through taxation people and companies with higher earnings.

Secondly, my administration is an adult one. For a long time we have had a Black percentage of 96 in our Government service—including police and magisterial personnel. For the past twelve years the whole of the internal affairs administration was in our hands. Officials seconded to us from the Republic will not disappear overnight with the coming of independence. They will stay on as long as their presence is required for efficient administration. Therefore, there will be no slackening of standards, chaos or unrest after the Transkei becomes independent. The conversion will, as over the past thirteen years, proceed smoothly.

Thirdly, the Transkei, which has already attained all her administrative goals, has only one overriding objective ahead of her, and that is economic development. Economic development must take two forms. On the one hand, our agriculture must be revitalised so that we can feed our growing population and, if possible, to export produce, and also to form the basis for secondary industry. On the other hand, secondary industry (and especially manufacturing) must attract those rural people who, as a result of agricultural revitalisation, must seek another vocation. It is obvious that agricultural development can and must form a cornerstone of my Government policy, and also that of any other Transkeian Government which might replace us. Notwithstanding those already in Umtata and Butterworth, it is the industrialists who hold the key to the future, and they can rest assured that they will be efficiently cared for.

At this stage I want to touch on a topic I feel strongly about: attempts to bar investment in South Africa, and the Transkei in particular. I denounced such attempts as "taking the bread out of the people's mouths" when I spoke on the subject on May 6, 1976 in the Legislative Assembly. I then said such attempts should be dismissed with the contempt they deserved. I was replying to a joint statement issued in Johannesburg two months previously by the Chief Councillor of KwaZulu, Chief Gatsha Buthelezi, and the Director of the Christian Institute, Dr Beyers Naude. I said the statement could be construed as condemning foreign investment in the Homelands and as a personal attack on me as I was a well-known protagonist of such investment.

> "For two well-fed, well-dressed and well-paid individuals such as they to preach virtues of mass unemployment would be hilarious if the potential consequences were not so serious". I continued: "To harangue the crowds on how Angola and Moçambique inspire Blacks in South Africa to throw off the yoke of oppression was bad enough. But to attempt to evade being regarded as an inciter by saying these

things merely as a friendly warning against eventualities they devoutly hope will not occur, is the height of cynicism. The two men had overlooked the fact conveniently that Angola and Moçambique had simply exchanged the Portuguese yoke for Russian and Cuban yokes. Pictures of the Angolan bloodbath and the food queues in Moçambique proved that liberation on those terms was literally a case of from the frying pan into the fire. If my critics saw the oppression of Blacks as an improvement of the lot of the Blacks, then their values were strange."

I concluded:

"I agree with the erudite speakers that Blacks in South Africa have for many years been oppressed. I only disagree with them on how we can escape this oppression."

BLACK-WHITE RELATIONS

In my policy speech in the Legislative Assembly on March 28, 1974, when I spoke quite extensively on Communism and terrorism, I also touched on this delicate subject. I said:

"Another matter on which I would like to express a few views is the question of Black-White relations in South Africa. This is a delicate problem requiring our honest and serious attention. In considering this problem we must be objective. Our attitude to other racial groups should not be determined or dominated by our emotions. We should not allow history to have a negative influence on our present or future thinking on this problem. I know, honourable members, that certain attitudes and actions of the White man in South Africa have caused, and are still causing, resentment amongst Africans.

"The most resented, I am sure, is the White man's attitude of superiority and all the resultant actions which flowed from this attitude. Let us look at this phenomenon a little closer. What gave rise to this attitude? In my opinion it started with the position which existed when the two races came into contact in South Africa. This attitude has, however, unfortunately become traditional and has not kept pace with the times. There are further, also unfortunately, amongst us those who, being unsure of themselves, have developed an inferiority complex which now seeks expression in thoughts of violence and aggression—those who want to show the White man what they are worth.

"The position in South Africa is such that neither Black nor White can afford to harbour petty feelings of hatred and revenge. White and Black will have to work out the future of South Africa together because we will have to live together on one sub-continent. We will be interdependent and if the future is to hold any advantage for any of us we will have to live together harmoniously. Neither petty grievances nor constant raking of past wrongs, whether real or imagined, will assist in any way.

"On the national level a great step to improve race and international relations has been taken with the summit meeting between Homeland leaders and the South African Prime Minister. In this way meaningful dialogue can in future take place. We will be in a position to discuss with the White Government those matters which we feel are hurting the dignity of the Black man in South Africa and also any other matter of importance to us. The reverse will, of course, also apply. This opportunity for having frank and honest discussions on contentious matters will go a long way to improving relations between White and Black in South Africa. We will, honourable members, have to readjust ourselves to our new circumstances under which there is no need for us to feel inferior. All of us will also have to make a determined effort to improve relations on the personal level and to educate our people at every opportunity towards this goal."

APARTHEID ... AND TERRITORIAL INDEPENDENCE

Apartheid is segregation. I've been long opposed to it; I've been opposed to segregation of any kind. I regret that this has ever been a policy in South Africa, because it has complicated matters now. I feel that if we lived as South Africans, and at the same time retained our areas where we lived without any restrictive laws about the movement of our people, relations in this country would have been very good. I don't think anybody would like to see integration of races in any way. It has not happened anywhere. It has not happened in America, in Great Britain. The national identity of all groups has been maintained. You find the Chinese people by themselves, the Jews by themselves and so on. That is the position which you find in this country. You find the Tswana people. You find the Sotho people. You find the Zulu people. Therefore I don't think it was necessary to pass legislation to maintain this national identity of groups.

I am opposed to apartheid. I am opposed to segregation. I think the people should enjoy human rights equally. Nevertheless, I also subscribe to the policy of territorial independence of people. That is the policy of the National Government of South Africa, of the Afrikaners. At the same time I reject the policies of the United Party and the Progressive Party, because these policies are designed to maintain White political supremacy in South Africa (including the Homelands) for a certain, undefined time.

In any event, we find ourselves in a situation where we have to seek independence because of the South African situation. It is the only way in which we can live happily in this country. I am convinced of this. When I took up this policy of separate development, I consulted no one, not even my colleagues. When I decided that the Transkei should be self-governing, I was convinced that this was the only road to the happiness of our people and the only way in which we could live in harmony with the citizens of the

Republic. Personally I don't feel the consequences of apartheid in South Africa because I am not subjected to petty apartheid measures such as separate entrances and the like, but I feel that it is not fair that my people should be subjected to petty apartheid laws. I wish these to be abolished. At the same time I am optimistic that we are moving in that direction already. I am sure that the Prime Minister of South Africa, Mr John Vorster, who is the key figure in the determination of policy, is moving towards that direction—namely the removal of these petty apartheid measures.

I also appreciate the fact only too well that Mr Vorster has a people to educate, and that it is impossible to force the people into this overnight. He has to educate them and with the help of his colleagues I am sure that he will succeed. Unfortunately one finds fanatics in every community; there are always extremists who pull the other way. In following this course I've been consistent over the years. As I said before, the policy of the Nationalists appealed to me since they came to power in 1948 because they came forward with a policy at a time when the Black people wanted to control their own affairs. And at that time the rest of the African people didn't approve of the National Party. More than twenty years later—at our Independence Day celebrations at Engcobo on December 11, 1968—I reaffirmed my support for separate development, but I also reiterated my criticism of racial discrimination. I said at the time:

> "Separate development had now become a reality, no longer an experiment, and was also a world pattern for solving race problems.
>
> "During the past five years, the Transkei had had its own Legislative Assembly and six-member Cabinet. These Black leaders have vindicated any misconceptions that the colour of a man is the yardstick in measuring his capabilities. South Africa was, and had been for more than 300 years, a multi-racial country. Neither of the races inhabiting this country is

prepared to sacrifice its own traditions, culture and national identity into a conglomerate blood mixture of an integrated society. Separate development is the answer to the question: How are racial clashes to be avoided not only in South Africa but throughout the world? The Transkei has chosen this road with determination to travel along it *ad infinitum*. The 'Doubting Thomases' should not stand in the way of our political liberation.

"We believe in the sincerity of Dr Verwoerd's policy which now remains to be carried out fully by his successors in the same party he led. The Transkei should cling to its ideals and continue building its nationhood as a separate entity. We should make the best use of what is in our power and take the rest as it happens."

Similarly, when asked by a BBC interviewer in July 1975 regarding the Transkei's relations with South Africa after independence, my answer was:

"I have no doubt that our relations with South Africa will be good because South Africa is moving away from discrimination. There are signs already that South Africa will certainly move away from discrimination."

TRANSKEI AND UNO, OAU

Regarding possible membership of the United Nations Organisation and the Organisation of African Unity, the Transkei is not trying to please anybody in seeking independence. It is our own decision, and we don't think any other person or body has the right to pass judgement on us. The independence is ours. We don't think any other person has the right to say that the Transkei should not become independent.

I made my position clear in a statement after the General Assembly's special political committee, approved by 100 votes to none on October 30, 1975 a resolution condemning

South Africa's establishment of tribal Homelands:

"It amazes me and my people that this organisation which professes to have the interests of the underdog and oppressed nations at heart should blatantly discriminate against just such a Black nation in Southern Africa, my people the Transkeians. If one is to be guided by the examples of Botswana, Lesotho, Zambia, Malawi, Uganda, Kenya and Tanganyika, I presume we would have been welcomed into the UN as were they. In this latest folly the UN Political Committee is, therefore, again manifesting the double standards which have become its hallmark. I understand only too well that the object is perhaps not so much to get at the Transkeian people but really to attempt to force upon the Republic of South Africa a policy of majority rule within the present borders of the country. But these selfsame borders of the Republic are artificial and remnants of a colonial past whose legacy is split nations and oppressed minorities. It passes my comprehension, therefore, why the anti-colonial UN clings to these imperial relics so passionately and rejects the Transkei which is doing nothing more than regain sovereignty over its traditional territory. At the same time the world appears sympathetically disposed towards the national aspiration of various other minority groups campaigning for freedom within the borders of larger nation states. The recent uproar over the Spanish executions of Basque nationalists is a good example. Here again there is no consistency in the world community's approach to nationalism.

"Clearly, therefore, the Transkei must expect no logic to be brought to bear on its forthcoming application to become a member of the UN. We shall, when the time comes, make such an application. If our brothers keep us out it will be to their eternal shame. But I have no doubt that significant member countries will not run with the pack and will stand up and be counted. Until wiser counsels prevail ... it shall be with those significant countries that the Transkei will conduct its legitimate business outside the hall of anarchy which the world body has become."

I would thus regard it as a sad occasion if the United Nations rejects our application, because we would like to participate in the solution of international problems. I feel, therefore, that the Transkei with its distinctive historical background can make a special contribution in this respect. But not every nation is a member of the UN, e.g. Switzerland which has always been a neutral country and has never sought membership in the world body. Notwithstanding Switzerland is highly respected by the international world. We shall remain in that situation and will maintain our integrity as a nation; we will try to develop our country with the assistance of friendly nations. We hope we will make friends who will assist us whenever we seek assistance.

If the Organisation of African Unity, our own brothers, decide that the Transkei cannot become a member of that body, to us Transkeians it would also be a sad occasion to be rejected by our own people, because we would like to participate in the solution of matters affecting the peace and good order in Africa. We also intend applying for membership of the Olympic movement. I am of the opinion that sport could make an important contribution towards bringing people throughout the world closer together.

A WHITE COULD BECOME PRIME MINISTER

When I said in an interview *(To The Point,* October 17, 1975) that a White person could even become Prime Minister of the Transkei, it caused some eyebrows to be raised. I would, therefore, like to explain this statement. The Whites will be welcome to remain and to own property in the Transkei as long as they become Transkei citizens. They may apply for citizenship and each case will be dealt with on its merits. A White person who is a citizen is also welcome to stand for election to the National Assembly, and could even become Prime Minister. But as far as I can see, the majority of the Whites in the Transkei want to retain their South African citizenship. Only the Whites who come from overseas wish to become Transkeian citizens.

Take the Whites of Port St Johns for instance. I had assured White residents and businessmen in Port St Johns that they would be free to remain in the town and carry on their normal activities. I said that my Government would neither exert pressure on residents to leave nor would any Whites in the Homeland be forced to take out citizenship of the Transkei. But as far as I can see, most of the White people of Port St Johns and elsewhere do not wish to remain. They wouldn't like to be Transkeian citizens even in Port St Johns; they wish to retain their South African citizenship. Naturally we would like the land to belong to Transkeian citizens only.

One further point: Whites who decide to leave the Transkei will receive adequate compensation for their vested interests from the South African Government. For the rest, I would like to assure the Whites that they have nothing to fear on the day of independence, October 26, or thereafter. White residents have expressed the fear in certain newspaper reports that matters could get out of hand in the excitement of independence. It is not our intention to interfere with the presence of Whites after independence, whether they are citizens of the Republic, or any other country for that matter. Our main interest lies in the development of the Transkei. As far as I am concerned, there can be no progress without technical assistance from outside.

I can also give the assurance that integration regarding churches and schools will not be compulsory in an independent Transkei. Education and the attendance of church services are matters which should be left to the choice of the individual. No one should interfere with citizens in their freedom of choice in these matters. If the Whites prefer White private schools and their own churches, they can have it. But in so far as Government schools are concerned, these will be open to all races. Other public places such as hotels and restaurants will also be open to everybody. The same principle will apply to sport. In the Transkei there are, for example, various clubs such as the Tembo Royals and the Pondo Chiefs, which were formed according to tribal affiliation. If the Whites prefer to have their own sports clubs, they will be free to have these. But any international team which will represent the Transkei must be open to everybody.

I can also state here that thus far no decision has been reached regarding the Immorality Act, and the relevant stipulation prohibiting mixed marriages. I leave this decision in the hands of the Minister of Justice. He is the man who will consider this matter.

I am also continually asked to provide answers to other questions that crop up from time to time, viz:

BORDER POSTS

We will have three border posts, namely at Kei Bridge, Umzimkulu and the Queenstown Road. We will also take over the border post at Qacha's Nek on the border between Lesotho and the RSA. The K D Matanzima Airport near Umtata will also constitute an international point of entry. I do not foresee South Africans being compelled to produce passports to enter the territory, as we would like to retain free movement between our country and South Africa. Our men are also moving continually between the Transkei and South Africa. We would not like to inconvenience them. But in general I should point out that there are always passport formalities between independent countries. Passports are a consequence of independence. Other countries will simply have to accept the fact that we are independent. Our constitution is a document which will determine our position, and which makes it clear that we are a sovereign state.

DIPLOMATIC LINKS

Immediately after independence we will have our embassy in Pretoria and South Africa will have an embassy in the Transkei. We shall have consular representatives in the various main cities in South Africa. As I have stated before, we have already applied for full membership of the customs union between South Africa, Botswana, Lesotho and Swaziland. The South African currency (the Rand) will also be in use in the territory.

FEDERATION

I am of the opinion that future political developments in South Africa might include a federation in which Blacks and Whites would be equal partners. I have no doubt that Black people and White people will live in this country on an equal footing. A Federation of the whole of South Africa cannot be ruled out.

ECONOMIC VIABILITY

Research by South African economists has reflected a promising future for the Transkei. The territory, the studies showed, was better off than 85 per cent of other African countries. The following must be borne in mind: The maximum annual per capita income for a country to rate priority aid was laid down by the United Nations as R143. Yet in the Transkei the annual per capita gross national income was R175, having increased from only R59 in 1960. Black families in the urban areas of the Transkei had an annual income of R2 338, which was larger than the R2 000 received by equivalent families in the Johannesburg area. Also, there are many sovereign countries in Southern Africa that are economically dependent on the Republic. Lesotho is dependent on South Africa, and so are Swaziland, Botswana and Malawi. Furthermore, there is not a single country in the world that is economically independent. All countries are interdependent economically. As far as the Transkei is concerned, that does not mean that we will have to fall under the Republic politically.

Lastly, while it is true that the Republic provided about 85 per cent of our budget in the past, when you consider the customs and excise duties and many indirect taxes that are paid to the RSA, you will find that the money which is being allocated to us by the Republican Government is largely compensatory for indirect taxation on goods consumed in Transkei and, therefore, our rightful due. We will continue to receive the yield of direct taxes paid by our citizens working in the Republic of South Africa.

TOURIST FACILITIES

The tourist industry is very important. We have a fascinating coastline and we intend building hotels along the Wild Coast. Another area of great tourist potential is the Drakensberg mountain range which borders on Lesotho. There are beautiful forests and fascinating scenery. Work has already commenced on a Holiday Inn in Umtata. We hope to have the hotel ready for Independence Day. I was given to understand that all the rooms were completely booked out before the builders were on the site.

RADIO STATION

After independence we shall establish our own broadcasting corporation. It will be operating from Umtata. In the meantime we will continue to receive Radio Bantu from King William's Town as broadcast by the SABC.

AIRPORT

The new international airport in Umtata will be called the K D Matanzima Airport and will be open by independence. The Transkeian Airways Corporation will by that date be operating a daily scheduled jet-prop flight to Jan Smuts Airport.

HARBOUR DEVELOPMENT

I think we can have a harbour along our coast, not necessarily at Port St Johns, because many people say there is a whirlpool at Port St Johns and so it might not be suitable. But there must be a harbour. We'll leave that to the experts in the building of harbours; we will ask engineers to investigate the most suitable site. We have several rivers flowing into the sea where a harbour could be established. Coffee Bay is a possibility, also the Umgazi river mouth in the event of Port St Johns being unsuitable.

POSSIBLE AMALGAMATION BETWEEN THE TRANSKEI AND CISKEI

That is a matter which we feel depends on the Ciskei. As far as we are concerned, we invited them a long time ago to join us ... we will leave it to them to decide.

BLACK UNREST

The riots on the Reef and elsewhere in the country since June 1976, in my view, demonstrated victimization of Blacks and vindicated the Transkei's decision to become independent. I advise South Africa to grant unqualified equality to all races. My Government strongly condemns the use of guns by police on young Black students who had acted no differently from White students at Rhodes and the Witwatersrand universities. After consultation with my Cabinet on my return from abroad I issued the following statement:

> "We regret what is happening as a result of a system of education applied forcibly against their expressed protestations. We advise the Government of South Africa to repeal all discriminatory laws and grant unqualified equality to all races of this country on the lines we propose to do when the Transkei becomes independent."

7

my land and its people

The Transkei is poised on the threshold of independence which, as I have tried to explain in the previous chapters, is the culmination of the policy of multi-national development in this Homeland. Because of the interest aroused by this event, questions are often asked about the economic potential and development possibilities of this country. But a country is more than just cold statistics; within its borders it is the heartbeat of a nation which keeps it going; it is the very life of its people which breathes over the grasslands and mountain valleys that is the spiritual dynamo of the development of a nation. The spirit of the land and its people combine to unite the urban and rural complexes ... it unites the herdsman in the veld and the businessman in the city so that they stand together in their mutual love for the land. It is in this spirit that I would like to give a short summary of my country and its people.

The Transkei is one of the most attractive parts of South Africa, consisting of well-watered undulating country rising from sea-level to an altitude of about 1 800 metres, and intersected by a number of perennial rivers, some of which have carved deep valleys, creating beautiful scenery. No part of the Transkei gets less than 500 mm of rain annually, and the rainfall of three-quarters of the territory is over 760 mm. The climate at the coast is sub-tropical, but it is mild at the higher altitudes. The climate is one of the healthiest in South Africa and is suitable for extensive agriculture. The average summer temperature is about 22 degrees C in the Matatiele district. Winter temperatures near the coast are as high as 15 degrees C while inland they range around 7 degrees C. The soil, in general, is fertile and the average rainfall of 762 mm per annum makes conditions suitable for the cultivation of maize, wheat, sisal and even tea. There is also enough grazing for livestock. Almost 19 per cent of the land is arable. This figure is considerably higher than the average for South Africa as a whole.

Before consolidation and the cession of Herschel and Glen Grey, this Homeland consisted of two blocks and is situated in the South-eastern part of South Africa between 30^0 and 33^0 S lat. and 27^0 and 30^0 E long. Before consolidation the Homeland covered an area of 3 855 692 ha. Natural boundaries are formed by the Indian Ocean to the east, the Umtamvuma River to the north, the Great Kei River to the south and the Drakensberg Mountains to the west which separate the Transkei from Lesotho. There are two main types of vegetation running in belts parallel to the coast: the eastern coastal bushveld and the sour grassveld of the interior. One also finds valley bushveld in the deep valleys. Because of the high rainfall, there are many perennial rivers. Among them are the Umtamvuma, Umzimvubu, Umtata, Bashee and the Great Kei.

POPULATION

According to the 1970 census, the latest figures available, the Transkei-Xhosa was the second largest group in South Africa with a de jure population of 2 978 240, of whom 1 410 520 (47,4 per cent) were males. A total of 1 644 640 Xhosa were living in the Transkei, constituting 55,2 per cent of the de jure Xhosa population of the Transkei, and 1 708 640 were living in White areas, which constitutes 43,7 per cent of the total de jure Xhosa population (Transkei 2 978 240. Ciskei 934 580). An exact distinction between Transkeian and Ciskeian Xhosa in both White areas and other Homelands is not possible, since the population census was based on home language.

Apart from the 1 644 640 Xhosa in the Transkei, there

were a further 83 600 other Blacks in the territory. The most important non-Xhosa in the Transkei are the South Sotho and Zulu, while there were only 2 420 Blacks of other ethnic groups in the Transkei.

Of the Transkeian Xhosa not living in the Transkei, 20 900 (mostly migrant workers) lived in Bophuthatswana and 12 900 in KwaZulu, while a further 2 500 were in Lebowa. Only 1,2 per cent of the Transkeian Xhosa were living in other Homelands. The non-Blacks in the Transkei constituted only 1,0 per cent of the de facto population and amounted to 17 752, of whom 10 097 were Whites, 7 645 Coloureds and ten Indians. The distribution of the 1 708 640 Xhosa living in White areas, indicates that 63,5 per cent were living in the Cape, 21,2 per cent in the Transvaal, 10,6 per cent in the Free State and 4,7 per cent in Natal. There was thus a wide distribution of Xhosa in White areas.

Only a very small percentage of the Xhosa in the Transkei live in towns. According to the 1970 census only 2,6 per cent were urbanised. This Homeland has one of the smallest town settlement programmes of all Homelands, mainly because various White towns were taken over and this eliminated the need for new towns and shopping centres.

AGRICULTURAL DEVELOPMENT

Cattle and sheep farming as well as the production of mealies, grain sorghum and legumes under dry land cultivation are the most important agricultural activities in the Transkei. Because our people are essentially farmers, we are hoping to develop agriculturally, and also hope that industry will develop side by side with farming. I am particularly optimistic about the potential of the Transkei's agricultural sector, to which about 80 per cent of the economically active population belongs. In 1973, 18,5 per cent of the total area of the Transkei could be used for the cultivation of dry-land crops. Almost 87 per cent of the dry-land arable land was utilised. Irrigable land comprises

2 348 ha, of which 75 per cent is utilised.

The R6-million Qamata Irrigation Scheme in the St Marks district is already irrigating more than 1 285 ha and a start has been made with a second and even larger scheme on the Ncora plains. A third irrigation scheme has been established at Malenge in the Umzimkulu district. Water for the Qamata Irrigation Scheme is supplied by the Lubisi Dam which has a capacity of 156 000 000 m^3. The dam is already full. When the scheme is fully developed, 3 000 farmers will be settled in that area. Crops include maize, wheat, lucerne, beans, potatoes, groundnuts and peas. The 250 ha Malenge irrigation scheme is in the Umzimkulu district and supports 160 farmers. There is a dam on the Tsomo River which will supply water for 5 700 ha. Part of this scheme has already been completed. We are planning a comprehensive hydro-electric scheme which is going to dam up all the Transkeian rivers lending themselves thereto. That will give us power generation throughout the Transkei, and will probably provide enough power for sale in the Republic.

Sisal is grown in the Butterworth and Lusikisiki districts on 1 790 ha. The XDC decortates the sisal at Butterworth and Lambosi for the bag factory at Butterworth. Tea grows well at Lusikisiki and Port St Johns. At Magwa, tea bushes have been planted on 783 ha and extentions are planned. A factory is already in production. Tea production in 1975 totalled 405 000 kg and was worth R620 000. In the Majola district near Port St Johns, 142 ha are under tea and extensions are being made. A factory will be built in 1976. At Lambosa, in the Lusikisiki district, 200 ha of Arabica coffee have been planted and a processing factory is to be built. There are also other smaller plantations. Pecan and Macadimia nuts are being planted in the Port St Johns district. Both these nut crops have great potential. Agriculture is under the control of the Director of Agriculture and includes training, conservation planning, specialised services, field services, information, physical development and co-operatives.

Traditional beadwork

Training

Two-day, in-service training programmes are held at three-monthly intervals at each of the district offices. Formal training is given by the Tsolo Agricultural College which runs a two-and-a-half year diploma course. The College owns 1 500 ha of land. The course includes cultivation, cattle breeding and field management, and covers lectures, demonstrations and practical work. Most of the students who graduate are absorbed by the Department, mainly as extension officers. The college can accommodate 100 students.

Conservation Planning

This section tackles soil erosion and sees to it that there is sufficient water for cattle. The farmers of the Transkei realise the need for conservation planning. The specialised services also promote scientific production and plan new projects and developments with the object of stimulating balanced and progressive agriculture. If we could increase our average production of maize to 15 bags per morgen, the Transkei could supply up to three million bags a year worth R100 million, or more maize than the Republic's annual consumption.

Extension Services

The aim of this section is to support and give leadership to farmers. It attempts to educate and create an awareness of the latest methods in agricultural production. The ultimate goal is to advance the concept of self-help.

Co-operative Organisations

Sixteen agricultural co-operative companies have been started in the Transkei. The co-operatives, which inter alia provide credit for agricultural needs, are also responsible for marketing surplus produce.

Animal Husbandry

A characteristic of the Transkei, which has already been called the future "pantry" of South Africa, is that agriculture and forestry play a secondary role to stock farming. In 1973-74 plant production amounted to 39,4 per cent, animal production to 57,0 per cent and forestry production to 3,6 per cent of the total gross value. Cattle farming makes the largest contribution to animal production, although sheep and goats also make an important contribution. The Transkei is one of the largest cattle-producing Homelands, while by far the largest amount of sheep and goats are found there. In 1973-74 the livestock figures for the Transkei were as follows: cattle 1 194 181, sheep 1 347 830, goats 1 330 312, pigs 320 232 and other ungulates 119 760. Various stock improvement schemes, dairy associations and agricultural co-operatives (membership 16 877) have already been established to provide farmers with advice, loan facilities and marketing channels.

Forestry

The South African Department of Forestry planted the first pine plantations in 1904. Since 1951, between 1 700 ha and 2 500 ha have been planted yearly. It was in 1963 that all plantations and indigenous forests were handed to the Department of Forestry and Agriculture of the Transkei. In March 1972, there were 112 plantations on 59 573 ha. Soft and pulp wood are grown on 32 of these plantations. The remaining 80 are used for firewood and poles. About 76 per cent is planted with soft woods. There are indigenous forests in the mountains and coastal areas. The mountain forests consist mainly of stinkwood and yellow-wood trees, while sneezewood and boxwood are found at the coast.

A total of 199 696 ha has been set aside for forestry, and of this area 178 984 ha have already been reserved for this purpose. In 1973-74 forestry production had a gross sales value of R1,4 million. Forestry has already given rise to the establishment of secondary industries. By 1974 four sawmills, employing 747 persons, had been established by the Xhosa Development Corporation which had also erected three furniture factories.

MINING

The Bantu Mining Corporation (BMC) is currently engaged in examining deposits of copper, nickel and platinum. Apart from the exploitation of travertine deposits near Port St Johns, which will shortly be started by the BMC, as well as a quarry which is operated by the Xhosa Development Corporation (XDC), near Umtata, there will be no other mining activities in the Transkei. During 1973 prospecting rights on 42 090 ha were granted to eleven private enterprises, but thus far they have had no success. However, we cannot rule out the possibility of discovering minerals. Who ever thought that the Free State was full of gold? We used to think that the gold was only in the Transvaal. The Transkei could also have minerals.

INDUSTRIES AND PRIVATE ENTERPRISES

Since we gained our self-government in 1963 we have made great strides in stimulating the economic development of the Transkei. Much of this is due to the Xhosa Development Corporation (XDC), which was established in 1965 by the Government of South Africa. The designated industrial growth-points are at Butterworth and Umtata. I am also happy to say that by Independence Day the Transkei will have negotiated an economic package for itself that virtually guarantees an indefinite period of stability. Before returning to the XDC, now succeeded by the Transkei Development Corporation, I want to refer to this most exciting development for emergent Transkei: the proposed investment by European industrialists.

Tea plantation, Transkei

As a direct result of my previous visits to countries such as Britain, the Netherlands, Germany, Switzerland and Italy, Europe's biggest spinner of acrylics, Bertrand of Biella near Milan, intends building a R12,5 million factory and plant at Butterworth, which will ultimately employ 2 000 workers. It has also been announced that a German firm is to set up a R1 million manufacturing concern, which will produce a new type of lightweight building material. Other ventures, either under construction or on the drawing board, include an Italian-run textile plant with a capital investment of R3 million, a factory specialising in the production of water purification plants and a process that will manufacture audio-visual equipment for training purposes. These industries will be located at Butterworth and Umtata.

All the businessmen I met overseas were very impressed by the Transkei's potential and by its political and social climate. I can define this climate principally as one of peace with a clear leadership based on evolution by contact with other countries. Such a situation is conducive to successful industrialisation. Regarding the Xhosa Development Corporation (XDC), it was started in 1965 by the Government of South Africa to stimulate the economic development of the two Xhosa-speaking Homelands—the Transkei and Ciskei. The main object of the XDC is to draw industry to the Homelands, create new jobs for the people, and so make the Homelands economically viable. In this programme the XDC is either the entrepreneur or it advances loans to industrialists who wish to take advantage of the concessions available in the Homelands. According to statistics, about R70 million has thus far been spent on establishing factories, plants, equipment, loans and infrastructural back-up. At the end of August 1975 the XDC was employing a staff of 6 000 of whom fewer than seven per cent were White. This does not include those employed in concessional activities.

Operations are widely diversified—the XDC runs 80 retail shops, 16 hotels, 14 garages, eight wholesale branches, fuel depots, bakeries, quarries and a plethora of other investments ranging from a brewery to cinemas throughout the Transkei. The concept hinges on the training and grooming of local citizens who will ultimately assume control of these various enterprises. In addition, the XDC is responsible for promoting concessional private industry under an attractive financial package deal. Currently this scheme has drawn a broad spread of industry from both the Republic and overseas.

The biggest private operating company in the Transkei is the textile manufacturing and retail giant, Pep Sotres, which has established a manufacturing complex worth R10 million and employing more than 1 000 workers. This factory is sited in Butterworth to the south-west of Umtata. Also in Butterworth is the food conglomerate of H Lewis, which has constructed a R1,5 million milling plant. The most recent industrial development is the establishment of the new Wispeco and Transkei Wire Industries factory. This dual venture will manufacture nails, wire and metal building supplies and will handle the sales of products associated with Haggie Rand and Wispeco Holdings. Total investment of the two projects adds up to nearly R500 000.

Umtata's biggest single manufacturing employer is Hilmond Weavers. Some 250 Xhosa women spin and weave mohair curtains and carpets for the company's three domestic outlets in Pretoria, Johannesburg and Cape Town. The XDC also claims that Hilmond, the gem of Transkeian industry, is fast developing a burgeoning export market. The success of this operation can be measured by the company's impressive growth in sales of 26 per cent in the past year.

I understand that the XDC plans to spend R83 million over the next three years to create 22 000 jobs. The budget for the current year adds up to R15,6 million. In 1976 this figure will rise to R32 million and, in 1977, R35 million. In addition, the XDC offers highly attractive concessions to bona fide industrialists:

- Loan capital at an annual rate of 2,5 per cent.
- Erection of factories at an annual rate of 5,5 per cent of construction cost.
- Housing rental for White staff at 2,5 per cent of construction cost.
- Railage rebate of 40 per cent on manufactured goods.
- A 25 per cent rebate on harbour dues via East London to a South African port.
- A cash reimbursement for moving costs from the PWV complex.
- A 50 per cent tax rebate on wages paid to Blacks during the first two years and a 10 per cent tax rebate on the book value of manufacturing equipment.

Private enterprises employed 4 007 Xhosa and 335 Whites as at March 31, 1974. (A year later the corresponding figures had already risen to 4 720 and 396). Most of the Xhosa workers, about 1 023 or 25,5 per cent, were employed in enterprises in the category civil engineering and construction.

THE SPIRIT OF THE COUNTRY

At the beginning of this chapter I mentioned that statistics could not do justice to the things that form individual people into a single nation. In my opinion the essence of this is summarised in the following description of the Transkei and its people by Mr Clement Mancotywa, an information officer in the Transkeian Government Service. In the mid-sixties he wrote:

> *A traveller through the Transkei is impressed by the beautiful hills, the forests, streams, and by the open country. He sees collections of cylindrical huts with walls topped and fronted with white-wash, and with conical grass-thatched roofs; sometimes he comes across Western styled houses. These are the homes of Transkeians called 'imizi'. He wonders what type of life the people lead, what they eat, what their difficulties are, what their pastimes are, and what they think. Do they view the landscape with the same aesthetic appreciation with which*

Forestry was started in 1904

he does? This cannot be denied when he hears the names of the places which have been derived from those of the rivers, hills, types of bush or grass, and so on—*Umtata (umthathi), Lusikisiki (sounds of reeds in breeze), Engcobo (a grass), Tabankulu, Tsomo, Mabelentombi, Mzintlava (a river), Tsolo*, to mention only a few.

But also the Transkeian might be looking at these landscapes more from the point of view of their usefulness to his type of life —shelter and grazing for his stock, water sources, sources of building material, fertile valley for his crops, and so on. The tourist needs to leave his car at the main road (it will be quite safe) and follow the footpaths that cut through the veld if he is lucky not to be stopped by rehabilitation scheme wire fences. Then he is in the heart of the rural Transkei and the picture he will get is of a pattern in any district of his region. The people are very hospitable, particularly to strangers, and all speak a dialect of Xhosa which is also understood by Zulu speakers. If he has been made conscious of it he may notice slight tribal differences in the different parts. Red blankets, long pipes used by both men and women, thick turbans used by women—in the Xhosa group (Tembu, Gcaleka, Mpondomise); scars on the face—in the Bhaca group; thickly oiled plaited hair, oiled skin skirts—among the amaXesibe; thin, long twisted hair, and circular beaded rings round the heads of Mpondo women. These tribal differences are predominantly noticeable among the illiterate, blanketed Transkeians. Many use European clothes which wipe out tribal traces as far as dress goes.

Occasionally he sees a woman or a group of women balancing things on their heads: carrying a bucket of water from the stream or spring, a long bundle of firewood from the forest, a gourd of beer to people working in the fields, a 'ngobozi' (basket) with fresh mealies and pumpkin from the fields, a bundle of thatch grass. Here and there he may come across men at their chores—fencing stock kraals or gardens with thorn branches, going with a span of oxen pulling a sledge with dry mealie cobs from the lands, or making poles or bricks with local trees and earth respectively. The girls are generally at the same chores as the women, and the boys go with the men, except that, in addition, younger boys will be seen herding stock. While the stock is grazing these boys play games which are associated with herding, hunting games and games designed to make them men.

He may meet a group of people going to a 'lima' (work party) to help a neighbour in his field or build a hut, or fencing, or any other task that needs many hands. The group may also be going to an entertainment or a ceremonial party— a wedding (patterns of European style weddings are generally found in tribal weddings), an initiation ceremony, a church revival meeting, or a beer gathering. The entertainments are plentiful when the period for work in the fields is over, in winter.

Life is very communal in the Transkei. The homesteads close together from 'Lali' (location) under a headman. There is a close tie between people of a location. It is a common thing to see children sent between neighbouring homes to ask for a bit of salt, sugar, tea, paraffin, milk or a bit of that. This is not interpreted as parasitism but rather as an expression of neighbourliness. Anybody who never asks for anything is considered stingy because he is debarring other people from asking anything from him. A visit to a home entitles one to two cups of tea or food. Any time is tea time.

At all parties, including Christmas parties, a lot of food, meat and drinks are served free to all and attendance is not only by invitation. The host generally does not know how many people will attend but the success of his occasion is judged by the big attendance. It increases prestige if people who have oxen plough for their poor neighbours or give them mealies to go and cook at their homes when they come to 'inkinkqa' (ask for foodstuffs).

When there is a death, neighbours are expected to dig the grave and to cover it up after the interment; also to bring foodstuffs to be cooked at the funeral. Talking about graves: Transkeians are very sentimental about the graves of their parents and grandparents and that is why they are reluctant to be moved from places where their homes have been for many years; they are not keen to leave their parents' graves.

Besides the richer folks that have put up Western style homes, a basic home has a great hut *(indlw'enkulu)* where father and mother and wives of married sons who have small babies sleep. A second hut is used as a storeroom and kitchen with a central fireplace. A third hut *(intanga)* is used by the marriageable daughters of the home. There may be a fourth hut used by a newly-married son and additional huts according to the affluence of the home. The people who may thus be found in a home are father, mother, their unmarried children, newly-married sons who have one to three children, widowed grandmother, dependents who are relatives (no matter how distant the relationship) and non-related dependents. The people who are not at home are the 'abakhwetha' (circumcision initiates). Special dome-shaped constructions *(amabhuma)* are made for them for the period of the initiation spent away from women.

The father is the head of the family and keeps connection between his family and other families of the clan. He may often be seen taking up his stick early in the morning and visit a member of his clan at some distant location to answer an 'uncimbi' (business); when people have come to ask the hand of the relative's daughter in marriage, or some such business. He also does not finalise clan affairs with his wife only at his own home unless the head of his house's clan is present. These people take their time to answer important issues. It reminds one of what Ngqika said when a White man came from Bedford to ask him for help. He told him that, 'I never sit by the fire until I have seen which way the wind blows'.

See two men meet. They greet one another by their clan names and their 'asking after each other's health' is itself a long conversation where they complain of the bad weather, diarrhoea or a cough of a baby, children's sores, their own lumbago, children's misbehaviour, a son who is in Cape Town or Johannesburg who has not been sending money, taxes, and a lot of other things. The strangers get the impression that this is a race of moaners who do not see any bright side of life. A passing group dispels that idea. They are forever singing in these groups at the tops of their voices like people who haven't a care in the world. Music of a type: with never any more

Hillmond textile factory

sophisticated accompaniment than a whistle or a harmonica. Some songs are wordless and have far more parts than the soprano, contralto, tenor and bass of Western music. The songs are full of rhythm and suited for work, walking, dancing, hunting, or just sitting or standing.

Some of the articles that the tourist buys along the road—baskets, carvings, decorated articles, clay pots, beadwork—are made at home when everybody is relaxing. The young men and big boys may be found at the local shop waiting for girls who have been sent to the shop to go and buy things. Men also sometimes go to the shop to hear the latest news about the next Great Place (KomKhulu). There have been constant talks of Tribal and Regional authorities, elections of Members of Parliament to go to Umtata, and 'Matanzima's Government'.

The changes have been striking to the ordinary Transkeian. A recent change has taken place in the 'mbizo' (meeting) at the Great Place (lomKhulu). Some eloquent, respectable men have been members of these government organs. They have seen local shops changing hands from White ownership to being managed by Blacks under what they hear is called the XDC (Xhosa Development Corporation). This at first entailed loss of credit facilities to them. They put all the blame on the failure of their own people and were fearful that they would perish should the Whites decide to or be made to leave. The picture has now become common: shops are Black, Black magistrates, doctors, lawyers, police station commandants, some villages are completely Black. The eyes of the Transkeians have now been opened to some advantages in having at the head people who can communicate with them without an interpreter.

There is talk of 'uZimele-geqe' (independence) which has been interpreted as the going away of 'abeLungu' from the Transkei. Whatever it is, and whatever 'secret ballot' means, the average Transkeian knows that he has been told about these by the Chief or the Headman. Chiefs have always worked for the welfare of their people. The education and Christian influence is known in every home because in every home, even though education is not compulsory, there is a child who has been to school. The standard of living—food, eating habits, *house furniture*—*is very high in many homes.*

But the trek to the cities will, in the years to come, probably also to a large extent bring an end to the mainly idyllic existence described above. It will mean the end of an era which future generations will remember with nostalgia.

8

my great love — education

In the first chapter I referred to my great love for education. This love was strongly influenced by my mother, Mogedi, who received no education herself, and from my father who, as a Chief, paid the teachers out of his own pocket, and after whom the Mlobo School is named today. I then also mentioned the fact that it fills me with quiet gratitude that I was instrumental in the establishment in 1950 of the first Secondary School of my tribe, namely the Matanzima Secondary School at Cala in the Xalanga district. Since then much water has flowed under the bridge.

You will, therefore, appreciate what a red letter day it was in my life when the University of Fort Hare, my old Alma Mater, honoured me with an honorary doctorate in Law in 1974. (Another member of Xhosa society, Mr J J R M Jolobe, at the time Moderator of the General Assembly of the Presbyterian Church of Southern Africa, was awarded an honorary doctorate in Arts.) It was the first time that a Black university had awarded honorary doctorates in South Africa.

Over the years the University of Fort Hare was served predominantly by students from the Transkei. A branch of Fort hare has since been established in Umtata, which will form the nucleus for our independent university, and the first students were registered in January 1976. The possibility of a medical school and an engineering faculty is a long-term one and, therefore, not foreseen in the immediate future. This institution has played such an important role in the history of the Xhosa people that I would like to dwell on it for a while longer. Fort Hare, adjoining Alice in the Eastern Cape, originally formed part of the Eastern Cape Colonial defences. It was named after Lieutenant-Colonel John Hare who established it in 1847, and from where many border campaigns against the Blacks were launched.

Many years passed, and the inauguration of the University College of Fort Hare on February 8, 1916 was the culmination of a persistent endeavour for the establishment of a central college for the training of Black teachers in order to create facilities for higher education for the non-White sections of South African society. As a college, Fort Hare had a very small and tentative beginning. The full-time staff numbered two and classes were held in a small bungalow. The college was incorporated as an institution for higher education under the Education Act of 1923. Although from 1924 the college assumed the dual role of a secondary school and a university college, it was possible since 1937 to concentrate on the studies of a higher education programme. In March 1952, the University College of Fort Hare became allied to its nearest friend and neighbour, Rhodes University in Grahamstown, approximately 70 km away. This association was most valuable in ensuring that its students at all times were on a par with standards that applied at White Universities. On January 1, 1960 the University College of Fort Hare was transferred to the Department of Bantu Education. This step became necessary in the implementation of the South African Government policy regarding the provision of more adequate and more effective university training for the Bantu. This university caters for the Xhosa-speaking nation. The university has grown to such an extent that it now has an enrolment figure of some 2 000. As from January 1, 1970, only ten years after the university college had been transferred to the Department of Bantu Education, the college was awarded full university status. Fort Hare is, therefore, in a position to adapt both the content of its curricula and the methods of presentation more effectively to the needs of the people it serves, without in any way sacrificing the high standards of a university education. I am fully convinced that this great institution will, as in the past, make an outstanding contribution to the further development of the Xhosa people.

PRIMARY AND SECONDARY SCHOOL EDUCATION

Regarding primary and secondary school education, it must be remembered that education was once in the hands of the church. It is, of course, now controlled by the Transkeian Government. The Transkei places great importance on education. In 1974, a quarter of the total budget was spent on education. The schooling of a pupil stretches over 12 years. Firstly, there is primary education consisting of a six-year course with the minimum entrance age of six years. Then comes the junior secondary phase which lasts three years. This is followed by a secondary phase of three years. For the first four years the medium of instruction is in the mother tongue. After that, up to university, English is used. Secondary education provides for academic, general and vocational courses. Differentiation occurs in Standard 8, where it is possible for students to select courses suited to their wishes and capabilities.

Blind, crippled, deaf or retarded children are educated at special schools or in classes which are subsidised by the State. One school is set aside for sons of chiefs and headmen. There are various bursaries available to children who need financial assistance to attend university. Adult education is conducted in 80 approved, registered schools. The main concern of these schools is literacy training. The latest figures available, those for 1974, show that the total enrolment of students and pupils in the Transkei was 489 213, of whom 486 178 were in state schools and 3 035 in private schools. The growth rate in school attendance from 1971 to 1974 was about seven per cent in primary schools, 12 per cent in secondary schools and 40 per cent in technical and vocational schools. New teachers are trained at six training schools, one college, and at the university of Fort Hare.

Number and type of schools in 1974

Primary	1 129
Secondary (Junior)	645
Secondary (Senior)	87
Training Colleges (Teachers)	7
Vocational Schools	5
Schools for Adults (Literacy)	80

The ideal has always been to staff an entire department with Transkeian citizens. From April 1974, to March 1975, much progress was made towards the realisation of this ideal in the Department of Education. In 1974 primary education was provided for 93,1 per cent of the total number of pupils, secondary education for 6,2 per cent and teacher training for 0,4 per cent. The number of pupils increased by 9,7 per cent between 1971 and 1974, compared with a growth of 11,9 per cent in the number of teachers during the same period. This means that the pupil/teacher ratio improved slightly from 60,5:1 in 1971 to 59,3:1 in 1974. The number of schools increased by 7,1 per cent during this period.

PROVISION OF SOCIAL SERVICES

Regarding health services in the Transkei, it was customary for these to be conducted basically on three levels: by clinics, mission hospitals and the reference hospital in Umtata. Clinics—each staffed by a staff nurse, two nurses and a general assistant—are found in the most remote areas in the Transkei. They treat minor ailments and the more serious cases are referred to a mission hospital. The clinics also perform an important service in warning the people about the dangers of malnutrition and give advice on how to avoid it. They are staffed entirely by Transkeian citizens. There are 22 mission hospitals which play an important role in health care. Each controls an area and is responsible for all health matters, including the clinics in the area. Most mission hospitals have equipment and staff for minor and major surgery.

When a mission hospital is unable to provide full treatment, the patient is moved by road or aeroplane to the main reference hospital in Umtata. The mission hospitals are registered with the South African Nursing Council for the training of nurses. The Umtata hospital has about 1 000 beds and 17 doctors. There are sufficient facilities to provide almost any medical care and the hospital is an important training centre for nurses.

The Transkeian Department of Health was established in 1873 (Proclamation R259 of 1972) to take over the activities of the South African Department of Health whose Homeland activities were financed by the South African Bantu Trust. The mission hospitals, which were autonomous up to that time, were also placed under the control of this department. Mission societies were compensated for their capital expenditure up to and including the transfer but the staff of the hospitals concerned remained unchanged. In 1963 there were 21 mission hospitals with 2 135 beds, while the number increased to 22 with 3 894 beds in the 1973-74 financial year. In the same financial year the Transkeian Government took over the St Patrick and Tafalofefe mission hospitals, which increased the number of State hospitals to seven with 2 169 beds. The total number of beds increased from 4 974 in 1972-73 to 6 007 in 1974-75, which means a ratio of 3,0 beds per 1 000 of the population.

Apart from the hospitals, the number of clinics increased from 71 in 1972-73 to 123 in 1974-75, a ratio of 0,6 clinics per 10 000 of the population. In 1974-75 there was a medical staff of about 1 810 inclusive at all the hospitals and clinics, consisting of 1 723 Blacks and 87 Whites. With the transfer of the Glen Grey and Herschel districts, a further three mission hospitals were brought under the

Jongilizwe School for Sons of Chiefs at Tsolo

control of the Transkeian Government.

PENSIONS

The amount paid in pensions increased from R5,8 million in 1971-72 to R7,5 million in 1973-74. Old-age pensions account for the major portion of the total amount paid in pensions, i.e. 69,9 per cent in 1973-74.

OUR NATIONAL ANTHEM

I can go on indefinitely quoting figures showing that great strides have been made in many fields over the past decade or so, but at the end of this book I would like to say something about our national anthem that is so near to our hearts. It is a source of pride to us that the song which has been selected as the national anthem of the Transkei—*Nkosi Sikelel' i Afrika*—was composed by a Xhosa member of the Tembu tribe, Mr Enoch Sontonga. Mr Sontonga was a teacher at a Methodist Mission School on the Witwatersrand in the latter years of the previous century and he wrote and composed *Nkosi Sikelel' i Afrika* in 1897.

Enoch Sontonga, a Xhosa member of the Mpinga family, had a gift for song. He constantly composed pieces, words and music for the use of his pupils at public entertainments. He wrote these down by hand in Tonic Solfa on odd sheets of paper, including *Nkosi Sikelel' i Afrika,* and eventually compiled them in an exercise book, with a view to printing them. This was in and around the years of the Anglo-Boer War (1899-1902). But he died before his ambition to see his songs in print was realised. Since then various teachers and choir conductors approached Enoch Sontonga's widow and borrowed the manuscripts, until eventually one friend disappeared with the collection itself.

Professor D D L Jabavu, the esteemed Xhosa leader of Fort Hare, confirmed all this in 1934 after he himself had made inquiries from the widow Sontonga and other members of the older guard who had known the poet personally. The stately song was composed in 1897 and sung for the first time in public two years later on the occasion of the induction of a Black minister in the Methodist congregation in Nancefield, near Johannesburg.

In later years the poet, S E Mqayi, supplemented the first stanza and refrain of Sontonga with an additional seven stanzas. The full text was published for the first time in 1927 in the *Umteteli wa Bantu* edition and during the same year the book *ImiHobi nemiBongo*. Two years later the hymn was published in the Presbyterian Xhosa Hymn Book *Incwadi yama-Culo Kunye neNgoma*.

The first stanza and the chorus begs God's blessing and protection. The other stanzas are devoted to prayers for the tribal chiefs, the public representatives, the women, the clergymen, agriculture and the labourers. Lastly, destruction is besought of all injustice in the land so that the blessing of the Almighty may rest on the land:

The full text is as follows:

NKOSI SIKELEK' I AFRIKA

1.
Nkosi, sikelel' i Afrika
Malupakam' upondo Iwayo;
Yiva imitandazo yetu
Usisikelele.

Chorus:
Yihla Moya, yihla Moya,
Yihla Moya Oyingcwele

2.
Sekelela iNkosi zetu
Zimkumbule umdali wazo;
Zimoyike zezimhlouele,
Azisikelele.

3.
Sekelel' amadol' esizwe
Sikelela kwa nomlisela
Ulitwal' ilizwe ngomonde,
Uwusikelele

4. *Sikelel' amakosikazi*
Nawe onk' amanenekazi;
Pakamisa wonk' umtinjana
Uwusikilele.

5. *Sikelela abafundisi*
Bemvaba zonke zelilizwe;
Abatwese ngoMoya Wako
Ubasikelele.

6. *Sikelel' ulimo nemfuyo;*
Gxota zonk' indlala nezifo;
Zalisa ilizwe ngempilo
Ulisikelele.

7. *Sikelel' amalinga etu*
Awonanyana nokuzaka,
Awemfundo nemvisiswano
Uwasikelele.

8. *Nkosi Sikelel' i Afrika*
Cima bonk' ubugwenxa bayo
Nezigqito, nezono zayo
Usisikelele.

GOD BLESS AFRICA (English version)

1. Lord, bless Africa
May her spirit rise high up;
Hear Thou our prayers
And bless us.

Chorus: Descend, O Spirit
Descend, O Holy Spirit.

2.   Bless our chiefs
May they remember their Creator;
Fear Him and revere Him,
That He may bless them.

3.   Bless the public men,
Bless also the youth
That they may carry the land with patience
And that Thou mayst bless them.

4.   Bless the wives
And also all young women;
Lift up all the young girls
And bless them.

5.   Bless the ministers
Of all the churches of this land;
Endue them with Thy Spirit
And bless them.

6.   Bless agriculture and stock raising;
Banish all famine and diseases;
Fill the land with good health
And bless it.

7.   Bless our efforts
Of union and self-uplift,
of education and mutual understanding
And bless them.

8.   Lord, bless Africa;
Blot out all its wickedness
And its transgressions and sins,
And bless it.

I reject allegations that *Nkosi Sikelel' i Afrika* is a freedom song that was heard for the first time at the Treason Trial (in the Republic).

Nkosi Sikelel' i Afrika is the Transkei's national anthem; it has the same meaning to the Xhosas as *Die Stem* has to South Africa, or *God Save the Queen* has to Britons.

In the spirit of *Nkosi Sekelel' i Afrika* it is my prayer that God Bless South Africa ... and that God bless the Transkei.

quotes by paramount chief matanzima

- "Communism is threatening the existence of all forms of democratic institutions. Self-development has now become our resolved policy and there is no turning tack from the road we have taken"—Chairman's address on the occasion of the opening of the third session of the Transkeian Territorial Authority on April 18, 1961.
- "We see ourselves as still being part and parcel of South Africa, sharing a common loyalty and being very conscious of the fact that our destiny and future prosperity are closely linked with and dependent on a peaceful and prosperous South Africa"—Foreword to the 1972 Transkei Annual.
- "Never in South African history has there been a leader such as General Hertzog. I have modelled myself upon his example. I am also fighting for my people"—Speech at Idutywa, *Rand Daily Mail,* June 11, 1973.
- "Our development should to a large extent be attributed to our excellent relations with the Government of South Africa, whose wise guidance, goodwill, co-operation, trust and material assistance have always been readily and generously available"—Speech at the official opening of the Xhosa Development Corporation pavilion at the Rand Show, April 22, 1975.
- "We have all seen two fierce dogs running up and down on opposite sides of a fence, barking, snarling

and threatening death to each other, if only the fence did not separate them. Suddenly, in their headlong rushing, they find themselves face to face at a gap in the wire. It is a moment of decision for them both—to fight or to move on to another intact part of the fence and resume their war of canine words. It is surprising how often the canine adversaries in that moment of truth, each sizing up the others' offensive capabilities, decide to forego battle and, albeit stifflegged and bristling in the beginning, to get to know each other, peaceable. Well, that is how I see the situation in Southern Africa"—Address to the Transkei Legislative Assembly, April 1975.

- "I am wholeheartedly in favour of the South African Government's détente policy. It is essential for peace and it must be extended to embrace the rest of Africa and the countries overseas. I still believe that the peace offensive is going to succeed"—Interview with *Die Transvaler,* June 30, 1975.
- "I am sure that the Prime Minister of South Africa, Mr Vorster, is moving towards the direction of removing petty apartheid measures."
- "We cannot have a people seeking freedom whilst slaughtering one another. You will not find that in the Transkei. The Transkei will become independent peacefully, and we are determined to live peacefully in our territory."